Introduction to Dinghy Sailing

Introduction to Dinghy Sailing

Nicolette Milnes Walker

DAVID & CHARLES
Newton Abbot   London   North Pomfret (Vt)

British Library Cataloguing in Publication Data

Milnes Walker, Nicolette
    Introduction to dinghy sailing.
    1. Sailing
    I. Title
    797.1'24   GV811
ISBN 0-7153-8022-2

Set in 10 on 12 point Times
and printed in Great Britain
by Hollen Street Press Ltd at Slough, Berkshire
for David & Charles (Publishers) Ltd
Brunel House Newton Abbot Devon

Published in the United States of America
by David & Charles Inc
North Pomfret Vermont 05053 USA

Contents

General Introduction

List of Illustrations

Introduction

Dinghy sailing is a marvellous sport. It has such great variety: you can sail very fast or very sedate boats, you can sail on the sea, on rivers, lakes, reservoirs and even canal basins; it doesn't matter how old or young you are; it doesn't matter how fit you are, or, within wide limits, if you have any physical disabilities—there are quite a lot of blind sailors, as well as one-armed and one-legged ones; you can spend as much or, nearly, as little money as you like; you can race in highly competitive fleets or you can cruise and potter around the country.

For me the attraction of dinghy sailing is the constant exercise of skill in controlling the boat and making use of the wind and water. You get a lot of sailing in a short time in a dinghy because you are always working physically and mentally to adjust to the continual change in circumstances. It is an active, exhilarating side of sailing, quite unlike my other love, long-distance yacht cruising, where you have all the time in the world, where things tend to happen slowly and where you may only change course once a day. For sheer boat handling I reckon you can get more out of an afternoon in a dinghy than you can in a weekend in a yacht. But it doesn't have to be like that; if you choose the right dinghy you can spend a lazy afternoon pottering round the creeks or lakes, doing a little fishing or just watching nature, though you must stay alert—dinghies react quickly to trouble and so must you.

In this book I have concentrated on the actual sailing of dinghies. This is because I think that this is the best use of the available space. Many beginners' books cover so many aspects of being a boat owner that they have little room to discuss how to sail a boat. I have aimed at giving sufficient detail for the large number of sailors who have mastered the basic skills of sailing as well as explaining the fundamental principles to the novice.

I would like to make it clear to the beginner that this book is in no way a substitute for experience in boats. It is meant to be a companion to practical learning, to help you to understand why the boat did what it did and what you can and cannot do to change things.

As well as the information about sailing the boat in various conditions I have included quite a lot on the practical problems of sailing, manoeuvring to approach and leave shore, anchoring and so on, on the basis that these are problems which frequently occur and to which there is a right approach which can save a lot of mess-ups and blushes. Not that anyone ceases to make mess-ups, particularly at the beginning of the season when you are out of a seamanlike habit of thought, but if you know the right way you are less likely to make the most obvious mistakes.

I have also put in a fair bit about the behaviour of wind and current so that you will be able to make the best use of them and will appreciate why a less obvious course of sailing may well be a more efficient one, and even a safer one.

The two chapters on racing are intended only as an introduction to a complex subject. I have tried to include the right amount of detail for the beginner and occasional racer so that they will be able to enjoy themselves without spoiling the enjoyment of their keener competitors. If you really get enthusiastic about racing you should get stuck into the more specialized books.

Now for the things that I have left out.

First of all, where to sail. In my opinion it is important to decide where to sail before you decide what sort of boat to sail. It is possible to sail without joining a sailing club by taking your boat to a public launching place. There is a book published each year called *Getting Afloat* which lists all the places where you can launch your boat in Britain. However, all organized sailing takes place under the auspices of sailing clubs, most of which are affiliated to the Royal Yachting Association which is the governing body for sailing in the U.K. Unless you belong to such a sailing club you will not be able to join any organized events such as races or rallies. The membership fees for most dinghy clubs are quite modest and for this you will get the use of a clubhouse, access to the knowledge and advice of experienced sailors, access to both social and sailing events and possibly somewhere to keep your boat near the water. The RYA publishes a booklet listing the names and addresses of all the affiliated clubs and their secretaries. This will help you to find out what clubs are within reach of you and you can then go and see what sort of sailing they are doing.

Having decided which club, or clubs, you want to join, ring up the secretary and find out, first, whether they have any vacancies—most will, but a few get full up now and then—and second, what sort of boats they sail. Most clubs sail several classes of boat, usually a beginners' boat such as the Mirror dinghy and several others of varying degrees of performance. Most clubs do not mind if you sail another sort of boat and many run handicap races for the boats which do not have class races but I think that it is better to sail a class which has its own races as you will be able to compare yourself more nearly with the others and therefore learn faster.

Many people do not buy a boat as soon as they start sailing but spend a season or more crewing for other sailors picking up experience and discovering the advantages and disadvantages of the various classes. You can also find out about boats by reading the yachting press and by visiting boat shows. When you have decided what you want to buy look through the advertisements in the yachting magazines to discover new and second hand prices and when you go to look at boats, particularly secondhand boats, take a knowledgeable sailor with you if you can. He will be able to spot weaknesses and faults more effectively than you and will make a good Devil's Advocate.

Once you have a boat, look after it carefully and it will retain its performance and value much better than if you neglect it. Keep it covered from dirt and water and if you break something replace it immediately so that you won't be tempted to sail with it broken. If you have a trailer look after that and try not to use it for launching the boat as the water will deteriorate the wheels and bearings.

If you have never done any sailing before the quickest way to learn is to go to a sailing school, preferably one approved by the RYA. As well as learning the right way of doing things you will be thrown into the company of many other sailors and will learn from your discussions together. You can find out about schools from their advertisements in yachting magazines. If they are RYA approved, they should be O.K.

When you have learned the basics, keep on practising. All sailing is practice and each time you sail you will learn a bit more.

Part One

Essential Knowledge

A dinghy has three essential components: the hull, which carries the crew and holds up the mast and sails; the sails, which convert the power of the wind into a force propelling the hull through the water; and the steering gear, which enables the crew to guide the hull where they want it to go.

Anyone who intends to sail dinghies either as a helmsman or as a keen crew member should understand more or less how the essential components function. He can then appreciate why the various techniques of boat handling are as they are and how changes in the boat and his behaviour will change the way the boat sails. The functions of hull, sails and steering are discussed in Chapter 1. The modern dinghy and its equipment are described in Chapter 2.

It is also important that anybody who wants to discuss sailing with sailors or to read about it in books and magazines should know the basic language of sailing. Chapter 3 explains the nautical terms you must know, and the glossary at the end of the book contains a number of other terms.

Chapter 1

The Boat

The hull

The purpose of the hull is to carry the crew and to support the mast and sails. Its most important characteristic is, therefore, that it should float; that is, it should be lighter than water.

The simplest hull of all is a floating log but this has many disadvantages. It does not protect the crew from the water, it resists being pushed through the water, it is difficult to steer and, perhaps most important, it does not have lateral stability but will rotate round its long axis, tipping the rider into the water. Nevertheless, some modern sailing boats are developed versions of the floating log: for example the sailing surfboard and the catamaran, which is formed of two enclosed hulls joined by a superstructure which carries the crew and sails. The hulls of these boats have been modified to improve speed through the water and to increase stability and steerability but they give the crew no protection from the water. However, it is more usual to have a hull which is a hollow shell, made watertight, so that it can be wider and more stable as well as protecting the crew.

In addition, it has been found that a long, symmetrical shape with a pointed front moves forward more easily than any other shape, although the best underwater shape for any hull is still a matter for argument and experiment.

To encourage the hull to move forwards and not sideways a thin, flat piece of wood or metal is attached along the bottom of the hull. If this piece is weighted and attached permanently it is called a keel. If it is not weighted and can be raised and lowered through a slot in the hull it is called a centreboard. Because the centreboard resists being pushed sideways the hull will tend to slide forwards when it is pushed even if the push is at an angle to the direction in which the boat is pointing, just as a child's scooter moves forward when the child pushes the ground with his foot.

There are a number of characteristics of a hull which are affected by the way in which it is designed. Buoyancy and stability affect the way the hull floats in still water and are known as static characteristics. Frictional resistance and residual resistance are characteristics which are only evident when the boat is moving and are known as dynamic characteristics. I will discuss these four characteristics in turn.

Fig. 1 More water is displaced by heavier objects: (a) *light hull unladen* (b) *laden hull* (c) *heavy hull*

BUOYANCY

A body which is floating in a liquid is buoyed up by a force equal to the weight of the liquid displaced by the body. This buoyant force acts vertically upwards through the centre of gravity of the displaced water. (This is Archimedes' Principle, the discovery of which is said to have caused him to leap, dripping, from his bath and run naked through the streets of Alexandria shouting 'Eureka'.)

So a boat in water will sink until it has displaced an amount of water which weighs as much as the boat—it will sink further in fresh water which is less dense than sea water. For this reason, the weight of the boat is described as its displacement.

When a boat is made heavier it will sink far enough to displace that amount of water whose weight is equal to the weight added to the boat. Similarly, for the same volume of hull, a heavily built boat will be less buoyant than a light boat. A light hull has the additional advantages that less of the hull is submerged, so water drag is less and it is easier to change the direction in which it moves, i.e. it is more manoeuvrable than a heavy hull.

4

The trim of a boat is the position it takes up when it is motionless in calm water. The stability is its tendency to return to this position when it has been moved from it by wind, sea or anything else. As I have said, the force buoying up the boat acts through the centre of gravity of the displaced water. This is called the centre of buoyancy. The force down, which is equalled by the force up, is the weight of the boat which acts through the centre of gravity.

When the boat is at rest the forces up and down act in a straight line. As the boat heels over, the centre of buoyancy changes position as the shape of the displaced water changes because the shape of the sub-

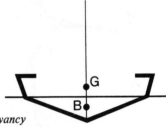

Fig 2 G: centre of gravity; B: centre of buoyancy

merged part of the hull changes. However, the centre of gravity of the hull stays in the same place in the hull. The forces through the two centres no longer act in a straight line but now try to turn the boat.

If you imagine that the centre of buoyancy is a hinge about which the boat is turning you can see that so long as the centre of gravity is closer to the bottom of the boat than is the centre of buoyancy the weight of the boat will pull it upright. However, as soon as the centre of buoyancy is closer to the bottom than the centre of gravity the weight will pull the boat over into a capsize.

When a dinghy heels over the crew move the centre of gravity of the boat (and its contents) by moving their weight so that the leverage of the boat and crew acting through the new centre of gravity with the centre of buoyancy as a pivot, exactly counteracts the leverage exerted on the boat by the wind pushing the sails.

Because the position of the centre of buoyancy depends on the position of the displaced water the shape of the hull will affect its stability. A broad hull will be more stable than a narrow one.

If the hull contains a lot of bilge water, water which is slopping about

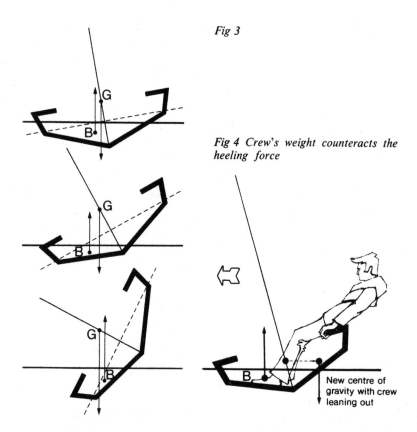

Fig 3

Fig 4 Crew's weight counteracts the heeling force

New centre of gravity with crew leaning out

in the bottom of the boat having been splashed aboard, the centre of gravity will change its position as the boat heels and the water runs from side to side. In extreme cases it can capsize a boat by moving the centre of gravity so far over that it is further out than the centre of buoyancy.

The longitudinal, or fore-and-aft, trim of a boat is not crucial for stability unless it is so bad that water flows in over bows or stern. However, it does affect the performance of the boat quite considerably, as hulls are designed to sail in a particular attitude. The fore-and-aft trim is altered by the crew moving forward or aft but it is difficult to check as if you lean over to look you upset the trim.

Fig 5 A broad hull is more stable than a narrow one

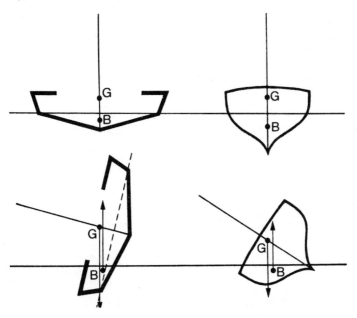

FRICTIONAL RESISTANCE

When a boat moves through the water there is a resistance to its motion caused by the friction of the water on the underwater surface of the hull. This is due to the viscosity of the water, but is greatly affected by the smoothness of the bottom of the boat. (The old sailing ships were often reduced to an amble by the weed growing on the bottom.)

The frictional resistance increases roughly as the square of the speed of the boat through the water so that it is twice as high at 2 knots as at 1 knot and sixteen times as high at 4 knots. Getting a really smooth bottom finish is therefore really worth while for any sailor and absolutely essential for the racing owner. The frictional resistance is also directly proportional to the area of the hull in contact with the water, the wetted area, and so racing boats are made very light to reduce this as much as possible.

7

This is the resistance of the water to being pushed aside by the hull. The faster the boat goes the more the water resists it. The disturbance of the water causes waves to form alongside the length of the hull. The first crest forms just behind the bows and the second one at a distance, d, from the first, where d is given by the formula:

d=(V)²/1.2, d in feet, V in knots

or d=(V)²/2.2, d in metres, V in knots.

Fig 6 Waves formed by a hull pushing through the water

Fig 7 Wave pattern at maximum hull speed

When the distance between the crests is the same as the waterline length (L) of the boat, there is a crest at the bow and a crest at the stern. If the speed increases a bit more the second crest leaves the stern and a huge trough forms. The resistance to movement is enormously increased and more power gives practically no more speed. The speed V_c, when the distance between crests equals the waterline length of the boat, is known as the critical speed and is given by $V_c=1.2\sqrt{L}$. It is the maximum speed you can expect from a boat floating on the water.

However, if the boat is light and flat-bottomed the water may give it dynamic lift, similar to that given to an aircraft. The boat is then no longer floating in the water but is lifted on to the surface where it can travel much faster because both the frictional resistance and the residual resistance are much less because very little of the hull is submerged. This is called planing.

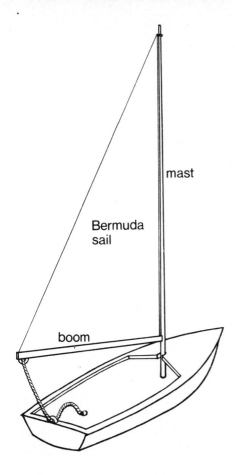

mast

Bermuda
sail

boom

Fig 8 Simple fore-and-aft sail

The sails

The purpose of the sails is to propel the hull in a desired direction, using the force of the wind.

The simplest sail is a large sheet of material which is hoisted above the hull and is pushed by the wind, as was the square sail on the *Kon-Tiki* raft. This type of sail is useful only for sailing in roughly the same direction as the wind is blowing. Modern sails are designed to take up an aerodynamic shape which can transfer the force from the wind into movement of the boat towards the direction from which the wind is blowing, i.e. to sail into the wind as well as being pushed downwind.

The simplest modern dinghy rig is a single Bermuda (sometimes called Marconi) sail. This is a tall sail, approximately triangular, which is stretched between two poles, the mast, which is fixed vertically to the hull, and the boom which is hinged at right angles to the mast. A

9

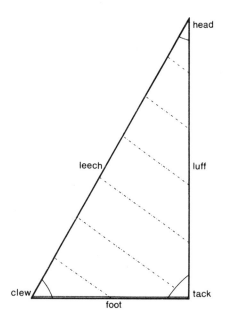

Fig 9 Parts of a sail

rope, called a sheet, is attached to the free end of the boom so that the angle of the sail to the hull can be adjusted. The various parts of the sail have their own names as shown in Fig. 9.

When the sail is left to swing freely in the wind the wind blows equally down both sides of the sail which lines up in the direction the wind is coming from, like a weathercock, flapping, or slatting, in the gusts. The wind exerts little force on it.

If, however, the sheet is pulled so that the sail is at an angle to the wind, the wind will blow it out from one side, exerting a considerable force. This force acts approximately at right angles to the direction of the sail regardless of the direction from which the wind is blowing. Knowledge of this important fact makes it much easier to understand how to adjust the sails of a boat, a subject which is discussed in Chapter 6.

If the wind is blowing from behind the boat it will push the boat forward and the boat is said to be running. If the wind is blowing from the side of the boat there is a force at right angles to the sail which can be thought of as being composed of two forces, one making the boat go forwards, the other making it go sideways. However, since the shape of the hull and the centreboard resist sideways movement the sideways force has little effect except to try to tip the boat over. But the forward

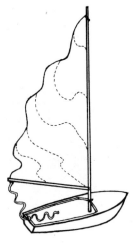

Fig 10 Sheet loose, so sail flaps

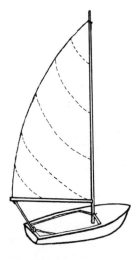

Fig 11 Sheet tight, so sail pulls

force will make the boat move forwards because the hull is designed to favour forward motion. If you press down on a damp piece of soap it will slide away at right angles to your pressure in the same way that a boat slides through the water when the wind is pressing on the sails from the side. The boat is said to be 'reaching' when it is sailing with the wind coming from the side.

For winds coming from in front of the boat the shape of the sail is important for getting the boat to move forward. As the angle of

11

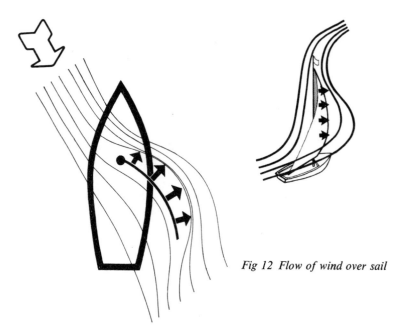

Fig 12 Flow of wind over sail

the wind to the boat decreases the push forward becomes very small compared with the push sideways. If the sail is completely flat the boat will not move forwards, but modern sails are designed to have a curved shape rather like that of an aircraft wing on its side. As wind blows over the curve aerodynamic 'lift' is generated which pulls the boat forward. A similar effect is shown if you put the back of a spoon into a stream of water from a tap. As soon as the water runs on the back the

Fig 13 Spoon is 'lifted' into the stream of water

spoon is dragged bodily into the stream of water. With both aircraft wings and sails the slower the speed of the airflow the greater the curve needed to generate lift: for this reason dinghy sailors alter the shape of their sails for different wind strengths.

Wind tunnel studies have shown that a sail generates the greatest lift when the wind is striking it at about 22° to the chord of the sail (the line across the curve of the sail). With angles greater or less than this the lift falls off, which is why dinghy sailors continually adjust their sails to get the optimum angle. As the wind moves further round towards the bows of the boat, therefore, the lift decreases until it is no longer sufficient to move the boat forwards. Usually it is not possible to sail closer to the wind than about 45° from dead ahead, but the exact angle depends on the boat, sails, crew, wind and water conditions. When the boat is sailing as close to the wind as possible it is said to be beating or sailing close-hauled. To reach a point ahead of the boat it will be necessary to make a series of zig-zags. This is called tacking into the wind.

If there are two sails on a boat, one on the mast, the mainsail, the other suspended between the top of the mast and the bow of the boat, the jib, there will, of course, be an extra driving force forward due to the increased area of sail presented to the wind. However, there is an additional force due to the effect of the jib on the flow of air over the

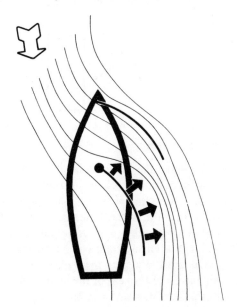

Fig 14 'Slot effect' of two sails

mainsail. The air is funnelled into the gap between the two sails and so it moves faster over the back of the mainsail. As the 'lift' generated by the mainsail is greater when the wind speed is higher this funnelling of air gives an extra driving force to the boat. This is known as the slot effect. Study of the effects of the width of the slot and the amount of overlap between the sails has helped boat designers to make modern sailing boats very efficient. Most dinghies have two sails, although there are a number of single-sailed classes for single-handed sailing.

Just as the flow of the wind affects the sails so do the sails affect the flow of the wind. As described in Chapter 9, downwind of a sailing boat the wind is turbulent, and another boat sailing in this turbulent wind will find that it cannot sail well.

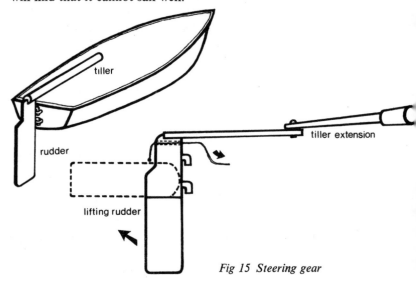

Fig 15 Steering gear

Steering gear

To make the boat change direction a dinghy has a moveable board suspended at the back or stern called the rudder. The angle of the rudder to the centre line of the boat can be altered by means of a pole called a tiller. In addition most dinghies have a tiller extension which is attached to the tiller with a universal joint so that the helmsman can steer even when he is sitting right out on the edge of the boat.

On most dinghies the rudder is made with a fixed part which is hinged on to the rear of the boat, and a moveable part which is pivoted in the fixed part and can be swung up out of the way of obstructions.

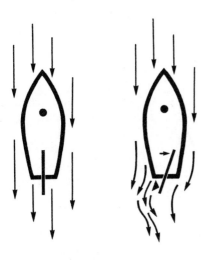

Fig 16 *When the tiller is pushed over, water pushes one side of the rudder*

The rudder affects the direction in which the boat goes by altering the forces exerted on the boat by the water. If the rudder is lined up fore-and-aft there will be little resistance to the flow of water past it. But if it is turned at an angle to the hull the water will press on it and swing the aft end of the boat round, (the pivoting point being the centre of lateral resistance of the boat; roughly speaking, the centre board). It is important to realize that the rudder has no effect if the boat is not moving through the water, for there is then no force exerted by the water on the rudder. Because dinghies have simple tiller steering it is easy to see that the tiller must be pushed in the opposite direction to the way the helmsman wants to turn.

Fig 17 *Push the tiller away from the direction in which you want to turn*

15

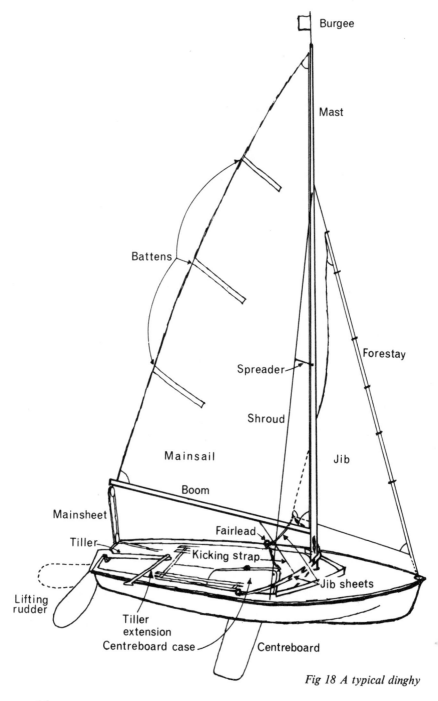

Burgee

Mast

Battens

Forestay

Spreader

Shroud

Mainsail

Jib

Boom

Mainsheet

Fairlead

Tiller

Kicking strap

Lifting rudder

Jib sheets

Tiller extension

Centreboard case

Centreboard

Fig 18 A typical dinghy

16

Chapter 2

The Modern Dinghy

There is enormous variety in the dinghies which are available today. They range from the traditional type of heavy, wide, undecked sailing boat through highly sophisticated racing dinghies and catamarans to the extraordinarily simple but strenuous sailing surfboards.

The extremes in size and performance of dinghies commonly sailed in Britain are the Optimist, a children's boat, at 2.3 metres long with a sail area under 4 square metres and the Flying Dutchman, the fastest Olympic two-man dinghy, at 6.0 metres long with a sail area, excluding spinnaker, of about $17\frac{1}{2}$ square metres. The most popular solo and two man dinghies are in the $3\frac{1}{4}$ to $4\frac{1}{2}$ metres (11-15 ft) range with sail areas between $5\frac{1}{2}$ and 11 square metres (60-120 sq ft).

Several methods of constructing the hull are used. In the past the most popular methods were clinker (overlapping planks), carvel (planks laid edge to edge) and moulded ply (strips of ply in crossing layers formed over a mould) and there are still a number of dinghies with these types of hull being sailed and raced regularly. However, later designs are almost exclusively made either from glass reinforced plastic (G.R.P.) laid over a mould or from planks of plywood. You can normally distinguish a plywood hull from a G.R.P. hull by looking at its shape. G.R.P. is easily formed into smooth curves with no abrupt changes in shape, whereas plywood is laid in sheets which join at an angle. These angles are known as chines. There are also a number of expanded polystyrene hulls coming on the market which are very light and buoyant.

The shape of the hull of all modern dinghies is similar. They have a pointed bow (occasionally cut off above the waterline which gives the appearance of a flat front), a hull two to three times as long as it is broad and V-shaped towards the front and nearly flat bottomed towards the back. The rear, or stern, of the hull is a flat vertical 'transom' on which the rudder is mounted. The transom will either have large holes covered with flaps or small holes sealed with bungs to allow water to be drained from the hull. The mast is placed about one third back from the bow with its foot on a mast 'step' which may be on the bottom of the hull or on the deck which normally covers the hull from the mast to the bows. Behind the mast is the open part of the boat where the crew sit, called the 'cockpit', which has either seats or side decking along the sides of the hull and may have a seat across the hull, known as a thwart.

Just behind the mast, on the centreline of the hull, is the centreboard, mounted in a case which sticks up into the cockpit. In some dinghies the centreboard is secured by a bolt at the front of the case and is swung round this by pulling by hand or with a block and tackle for heavy centreplates. In other dinghies the centreboard slides vertically up and down in the case and can be called a 'daggerboard'.

On either side of the centreboard case, attached to the floor, there will probably be toe straps, which are long wide rubber straps for the crew to hook their feet under to allow them to lean right over the side of the boat without falling out.

In the bottom of high performance boats are devices called 'self-bailers'. These are like small cups which, when lowered, stick out under the hull with their opening facing backwards. The movement of the boat through the water sucks out water from inside the hull. You have to remember to close them when you slow down or water comes into the hull instead.

At the stern the rudder is hung on pins known as 'pintles'. The vast majority of dinghies have lifting rudders and most of these are made from wood.

The mast is held in place by wires which are called the 'standing rigging'. On a dinghy this consists of three wires or 'stays' The 'forestay' joins the bows to the mast. It is sometimes attached to the top of the mast but usually to a point about two-thirds of the way up. The mast is held up at the sides by two wires called 'shrouds' which are attached to each side of the hull at points a little further aft than the mast, so that as well as stopping the mast from falling over sideways they stop it from falling over forwards. Sometimes the shrouds are pushed out from the mast about half way up by rods called spreaders to distribute their pull more effectively. The forestay and shrouds are attached to metal fittings on the hull called 'chain plates', and their precise length can be adjusted by means of a 'rigging screw'. This is a device which has rods at each end, threaded in opposite directions, one attached to the hull and the other to the stay, and a middle part with opposite threaded nuts at each end. When the middle is turned one way the stay is drawn nearer to the hull and vice versa.

The 'running rigging' consists of all the moving ropes on the boat. The mast is equipped with 'halyards' which are ropes used to hoist sails to the top of the mast. These ropes run through 'blocks', i.e. pulleys, at the top of the mast and are made fast to 'cleats', fittings with two horns round which the line is hitched. There will be halyards for each sail that is carried—main, jib and spinnaker (see p. 59)—and normally one of thin line for hoisting a flag at the mast head.

The boom is attached to the mast by a 'gooseneck', a fitting of varied design which allows the boom to pivot freely. The gooseneck is often mounted on a length of track up and down the mast and can be held in position either by a screw or a block and tackle.

From a point about a quarter the way along the boom is a rope called the 'kicking strap' which goes to the base of the mast. The length of this can be adjusted and its purpose is to stop the boom rising too high and, in high performance boats, to bend the boom to adjust the shape of the sail.

Either in the middle of the boom or at the outer end is the fitting for the mainsheet. This will usually be a block through which the rope runs from and to the hull. Across the top of the transom or, for a centre mainsheet, across the cockpit, there will be a track carrying a slide to which is attached a block through which the mainsheet runs to the helmsman's hand. On many boats the mainsheet runs through a ratchet block on the slide which allows the sheet to be hauled in freely but resists the sail pulling it out and so saves the helmsman from the continual pull of the sheet.

The jib sheets run from the clew of the sail, one to each side of the boat. They are led through round eyes called 'fairleads' attached to the side decks just aft of the foredeck. Sometimes the fairleads are mounted on tracks so that their position can be altered for different sails or wind strengths. Often they are associated with 'jam cleats' on the inboard side which are ridged spring slots into which the sheet can be jammed to relieve the crew of the strain of continually holding it.

The jib is clipped to the forestay by fittings called 'hanks' of various designs which are attached to the luff of the sail. The tack of the jib is attached to the bows by a shackle or a lashing. On some boats there is no standing forestay and, instead, the wire in the luff of the jib acts as the forestay.

The mainsail is attached to the boat at all three corners and along its luff and foot. The head of the sail is shackled to the main halyard, the tack to the boom at the gooseneck and the clew is stretched towards the end of the boom by a thin line. The sail is attached to the mast either by sliding the 'boltrope' sewn into the luff up a groove in the mast or by slides attached to the luff running up a track on the mast. Similarly the sail is attached to the boom by a boltrope or slides.

The loose side of the mainsail, the leach, is often stiffened by long narrow pieces of bendy wood or plastic called 'battens' which slide into batten pockets which run from the edge of the sail towards the mast. The battens stop the leach from flopping and help give a good shape to the sail.

You must remember that all classes of boat are different in shape and in equipment and while some boats of old-fashioned design have simple equipment and other boats of modern design have extremely complicated equipment there are, equally, new boats with equipment so simple that it hardly needs explaining and old boats with unusual and complex gear. The description in this chapter is, therefore, only a guide and you must not be surprised to find dinghies which are somewhat different.

Chapter 3

Important Nautical Terms

A sailor must know these terms so that he is able to describe what is happening. Apart from port and starboard, which are only jargon, but universal jargon, the others are the only terms available to define what is going on. It is important to know what they mean.

In sailing a boat, everything is related to the wind.

PORT AND STARBOARD

> Port = left (both are four letter words).
> Starboard = right, when looking forward in a boat.

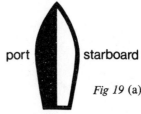

port   starboard

Fig 19 (a)

TACKS

Used to describe the direction the wind is coming from.

A boat 'on the port tack' has the wind blowing from the left-hand side of the boat.

A boat 'on the starboard tack' has the wind blowing from the right-hand side of the boat.

Travelling into the wind in a series of zig-zags during which the wind comes alternately from one side of the boat and the other is called 'tacking'.

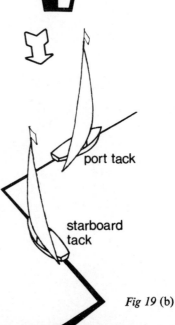

port tack

starboard tack

Fig 19 (b)

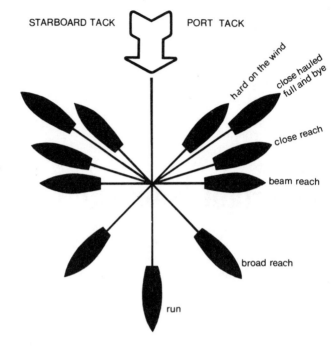

STARBOARD TACK   PORT TACK

hard on the wind

close hauled
full and bye

close reach

beam reach

broad reach

run

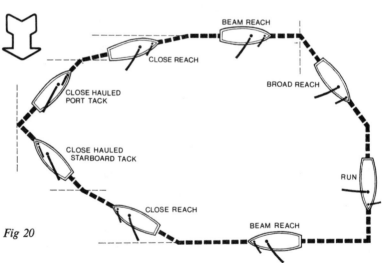

BEAM REACH

CLOSE REACH

CLOSE HAULED
PORT TACK

BROAD REACH

CLOSE HAULED
STARBOARD TACK

RUN

CLOSE REACH

BEAM REACH

Fig 20

On the wind. This means sailing close-hauled, the course sailed being dictated by the wind direction. If the boat's heading is as close to the wind as possible but the boat speed is reduced, this is called pinching. It sometimes enables one to get round obstructions. 'Hard on the wind' is as close as possible while still retaining a reasonable boat speed. 'Full and bye' is a little less close to make better speed. 'Off the wind' or 'sailing free' means being able to sail the course you choose. As the wind becomes further aft the point of sailing goes through 'reaching' to 'broad reaching' to 'running'. To describe the condition in which a boat is sailing the tack and point of sailing must be specified, e.g. close hauled on the starboard tack; broad reaching on the port tack.

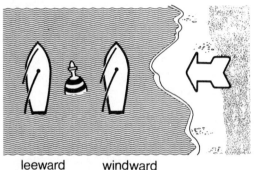

Fig 21   leeward boat   windward boat

WINDWARD AND LEEWARD

These terms denote sides of something, or positions of things related to the direction the wind is coming from. The windward side of the boat is the one which the wind reaches first; things thrown to windward blow back to the thrower. (Always be sick to leeward!)

The position of objects can be described two ways, e.g. with a wind blowing off the shore one can say either 'the leeward boat was farthest from the beach' or 'the windward boat was closest to the beach'. Similarly one can say 'I passed to windward of the buoy' or 'I left the buoy to leeward'.

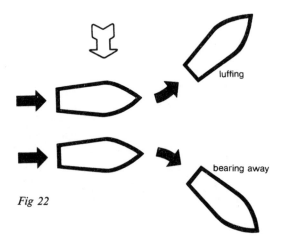

Fig 22

LUFFING AND BEARING AWAY

These denote changes in the heading of a boat relating to the wind.
Luffing means changing to a heading closer to the wind.
Bearing away means changing to a heading further off the wind.

Part Two

Practical Sailing

To sail a boat with confidence requires knowledge and experience. In this section I have included as much knowledge as a beginner can cope with without becoming hopelessly confused between the important basic requirements and techniques and the refinements which advanced sailors will consciously or unconsciously appreciate. This section is the meat of the book, but I do not think that it can be properly digested without the bread and butter of Part One. (Part Three is an optional dressing.) If you have skipped Part One, go back and read it now.

Chapter 4

Preparation for Sailing

Clothing

It is important to wear suitable clothes when dinghy sailing. Unsuitable clothing can be a nuisance and very uncomfortable, and can therefore make you less effective than you might otherwise be.

Many dinghy sailors invest in a wet suit which, provided it fits properly, can be comfortable and warm for the comparatively short duration of most dinghy outings. They are not suitable for longer periods. I prefer to do without a wet suit and instead wear an old shirt, old trousers—not so tight as to hinder free movement—one thin sweater, one thick sweater, an oilskin jacket and trousers and a neck-cloth to prevent water from dripping down my neck. Some people like to wear a one-piece overall oilskin, but these are difficult to get in and out of, particularly if you want to put on or take off sweaters. If you have long hair, tie it back or wear a woollen hat so that it does not flap in your face. For feet, wet suit socks are good, or canvas sailing shoes. Socks will get wet, but even wet wool will keep your feet a bit warmer. Plastic sandals are good because they let the water drain away, and some people cut holes in the toes of their shoes for the same purpose. Bare feet are not very good for they are slippery in the wet and if you use toe straps they will hurt your feet.

It is absolutely vital to wear a life jacket. There are a large number of different types available. Make sure that you have a life jacket that meets the British Standard requirements, not a buoyancy aid. I prefer the inflatable sort which you can wear semi-inflated.

In your pockets carry some spare codline (very thin rope), a spare shackle or two and maybe a spare bung. I also like a supply of boiled sweets or barley sugar; others may prefer beer and a sandwich or a flask of brandy. On a lanyard round your neck, or tied to your belt and kept in a pocket, carry a knife with a stout blade and a shackle key or spike.

Safety

Sailing can be dangerous and people do occasionally have serious, even fatal, accidents. These should not occur if you take suitable precautions.

The risks which you run in a small boat are capsizing, running aground, damaging the boat and, in tidal waters, being carried out to sea. Any of these accidents can occur through inexperience or lack of judgement, and the novice should not sail in conditions where such accidents could have serious consequences.

Firstly, do not sail when the wind is too strong. Most dinghies will not put to sea in a wind of Force 5 or above on the Beaufort scale (see Appendix). At this wind force it is difficult to handle a dinghy going to windward, especially at sea, and only the most experienced helmsman will try. Until you have gained experience you will be better off ashore in winds over Force 3 as things happen so quickly in stronger breezes.

Secondly, if you are sailing in tidal waters, make sure that you know in which direction the tide is running, how strong it is and when it is likely to turn. You must also find out at what states of the tide you can launch and return to shore. In places with a large tidal range it is often only possible to sail for an hour or two either side of high tide.

In light winds it is advisable to set off against the tide and return with it so that, if you are becalmed or otherwise unable to sail properly, you will be carried nearer to home rather than further away. Similarly in a river set off upstream and return downstream. In heavier weather it is a good idea to start by sailing upwind so that if the wind gets even stronger you will have a downwind sail home and will not have to beat into a strong wind.

Any dinghy sailing on the sea, whether racing or not, should carry a small anchor, say 2kgs. It should have three or four metres of chains to help the anchor dig in and about fifteen metres of rope, securely attached to the boat.

There are a number of internationally recognized distress signals. Those suitable for a dinghy sailor are: red hand flare, orange smoke signal, repeatedly raising and lowering outstretched arms or an article of clothing put on an oar, continuous sounding of a whistle or siren.

It is therefore wise when sea sailing to carry distress flares and smoke signals which you can buy in waterproof packs for dinghies.

It is essential to be able to empty any water from the boat, so carry a plastic bucket or bailer and a large sponge. Tie the bailer to the boat with a long line so that you don't inadvertently throw it overboard as well as the water nor lose it in a capsize. Carry a pair of oars or paddles and tie these down with line or elastic 'shock' cord so they don't float away if you capsize. In fact, tie down everything moveable and carry spare line in your pocket.

Knots

There are a few basic knots which every sailor needs to know. These are the Figure of Eight, the Reef Knot, the Half Hitch and the Round Turn and two Half Hitches. Two other knots are useful, the Bowline and the Fisherman's Bend and it is useful to know how to make a simple whipping.

THE FIGURE OF EIGHT KNOT

This is the knot to put on the end of ropes to stop them running through eyes and blocks. On a dinghy you will need one on each end of the jib sheet and one on the loose end of the mainsheet. It is simpler to undo when it is tight than the overhand knot.

Fig 23 (a) *Figure of eight knot*
(b) *Overhand knot*

a

b

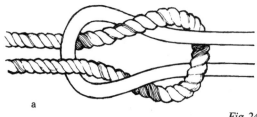

Fig 24 (a) Granny knot (bad)
(b) Reef knot (good)

THE REEF KNOT

This is used to join two lengths of rope of the same thickness. As you can see, it is a symmetrical knot, and holds well, unlike the Granny, which is liable to slip and should never be used.

THE HALF HITCH AND THE ROUND TURN AND TWO HALF HITCHES

The half hitch is for tying a rope on to something else, e.g. a post, a ring, another rope. A single half hitch is likely to slip, but two half hitches will probably hold unless the rope is slippery. To be sure that the rope is secure use a round turn and two half hitches.

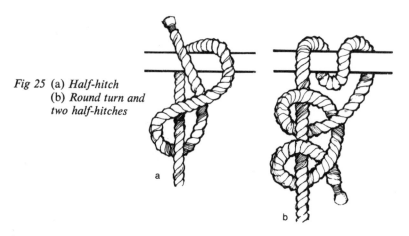

Fig 25 (a) Half-hitch
(b) Round turn and
two half-hitches

30

These are the most important knots for a dinghy sailor to know, but the bowline and the fisherman's bend are also worth learning.

Fig 26 Bowline

THE BOWLINE

This makes a fixed loop in the end of a rope.

THE FISHERMAN'S BEND

This is for tying a rope on to a ring or post. Unlike the round turn and two half hitches it will not jam when wet. This is the knot you should use for tying the anchor rope on to the chain.

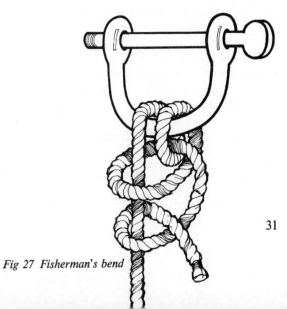

31

Fig 27 Fisherman's bend

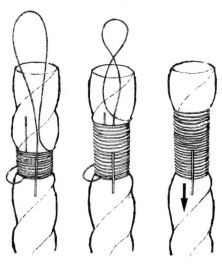

Fig 28 Common whipping

THE COMMON WHIPPING

This is put on the end of a rope to stop it unravelling. Use waxed thread which you can get from a chandler. The diagram shows the stages of whipping.

With many synthetic ropes it is unnecessary to put on a whipping. Just hold the end over a flame and the strands will congeal together.

Rigging the boat

We will assume that the dinghy has been stored in a dinghy park on a launching trolley. If you have brought the dinghy on a road trailer, transfer it to the launching trolley before you start preparing it.

The dinghy will be stored with a canvas cover on and perhaps with the mast lowered. The sails are kept separately at home in a sailbag, as is personal gear such as lifejackets, oilskins, etc. Some people remove all detachable equipment from the boat so that they are not stolen or the boat used illicitly. This is a wise precaution if the dinghy park is easily accessible to the general public, particularly at holiday resorts.

After removing the cover, the following steps are taken to rig the boat. Do not smoke while you are rigging or you may accidentally burn holes in the sails.

1. Remove any water which has collected in the boat and fit the bungs into the drain holes.
2. Raise the mast if necessary. The way you do this will depend on whether the mast is stepped on the deck or on the keel. If it is on the deck, attach the shrouds to the chain plates on each side of the

boat using a clevis pin. Place the bottom of the mast in its step on deck and have one member of the crew haul on the forestay while the other raises the mast by hand, making sure the foot stays in the step. Fasten the forestay to its bows. If the mast is stepped through the deck on the bottom of the boat it must be placed in position before the shrouds and forestay can be fastened. Open the gate in the deck, raise the mast to the vertical position and lift it over the side of the boat, tilt it aft a little and, with your crew helping, guide the bottom of the mast into the slot on the keel. Then you can easily tilt it forward into the space in the deck or thwart and close the gate to keep it in. Then fasten the shrouds and forestay.

3. The skipper can then adjust the rigging screws so that the mast is at the angle he feels will suit the conditions best. Usually only the keenest racing skippers do this every time.

4. If you have a burgee halyard, hoist the burgee.

5. Attach the mainsheet to the boom and boat and then attach the boom to the mast.

6. Turn the boat so that the bows face into the wind. This is so that the sails do not swing out to the side when they are hoisted.

7. Insert the battens into the pockets in the mainsail.

8. Attach the mainsail to the boom. It will either have slides which run on a metal track along the top of the boom or, more likely, will be edged with a bolt rope which is fed into a groove on the top of the boom. Fasten the end next to the mast to the boom with a shackle or a pin through the boom. Pull out the sail to the mark at the end of the boom and tie it to the eye.

9. Make sure the sail is not twisted. Fasten the head of the sail to the main halyard with a shackle. (The main halyard is commonly cleated on the starboard side of the mast.) Haul up the sail as tight as possible and cleat the main halyard to the mast by taking a number of turns around the cleat. Coil the loose part of the halyard, the fall, and stow it neatly either on the cleat or under the deck.

10. Fit the kicking strap. This usually slots into the underside of the boom and is rigged with a block (pulley) so that its length, and therefore its pull on the boom, can be adjusted.

11. Attach the jib sheets on to the jib, if they have been detached, either by tying a knot or with a shackle. Rig the sheets through the fairleads on the side decks, taking them outside the shrouds on most boats, and tie a figure of eight knot at each end.

12. Shackle the jib halyard, commonly cleated on the port side of the mast, to the head of the jib, and hoist the sail.

13. Hang the rudder on its fittings at the stern of the boat, making sure that the lifting blade is in the up position.
14. Check that the centreboard is not jammed in its case.
15. Check that the self-bailers are operating and are closed.
16. Stow oars, anchor and bailer, making sure they are tied down so that they will not fall out in a capsize. Stow spare clothing and other gear in a dry place, usually under the foredeck.
17. Stand back and check everything.

When you are sure that all is well, lower the sails, unless there is a very light breeze, so that they do not flail about while you are taking the boat down to the water. Then put on your oilskins and lifejacket. You are now ready to launch.

Launching

If there are plenty of helpers the boat can be carried to the water. Indeed if you are launching over soft sand, this is the only way. Put the boat either right in the water or right out of it, but do not leave it half in and half out as the boat will be rolled about and scratched if there are any significant waves.

It will usually be possible to use a launching trolley. Wheel it gently into the water so that the dinghy floats off it. One person can then hold the dinghy in the water while another withdraws the trolley and takes it away. The single-hander will usually find a willing bystander to hold the boat while he parks the trolley. If he is completely alone he will have to beach the dinghy and risk losing some paint off her bottom.

Hoist the mainsail, cleat the halyard, coil and stow the fall. Make sure that the boom end is not fouled up and that the mainsheet is not twisted and is running freely. If there is a boom downhaul, haul it down and fasten it.

Hoist the jib and heave the halyard taut, before cleating and stowing it. Check that the jib sheets are rigged correctly and are not twisting the foot of the sail.

A boat afloat and under sail can easily be held at the bows by one hand, but if you hold it at the stern or the side it will be very difficult to hold as the wind will keep blowing it round.

The way in which you depart from the shore will depend on the way the wind is blowing. We will return to this problem after discussing how to handle the boat afloat.

Chapter 5

Boat Handling

This chapter covers the factors which must be considered all the time you are afloat so that you get the best performance from the boat and do not get into unnecessary trouble. A detailed consideration of boat handling on the three points of sailing, beating, reaching and running, is given in Chapter 6.

Whenever you are sailing you must be aware of the following aspects of your situation: wind direction and force, sail trim, boat trim and heel, your position relative to the shore and obstructions.

WIND DIRECTION AND FORCE

You must always be aware of the direction of the wind relative to the boat as it determines how you set the sails and what course you can, or cannot, sail. When you have some experience you will be able to tell roughly from the behaviour of the sails but a beginner certainly needs some sort of direction indicator and, indeed, the keenest helmsman would be lost without one. Most dinghies will carry a flag, called a burgee, or a small windsock or windvane at the masthead. In addition, a tell-tale piece of wool or light cloth attached about a third of the way up each shroud is a great help. Of course, the leeward tell-tale will be affected by the flow of air over the sails, but the windward one will be in clear air.

The force of the wind can be judged both from sea and land conditions, referring to the Beaufort Scale, (Appendix, p.101), and, more relevantly, from the boat's behaviour. If the wind is too strong the boat will begin to take charge; the sheets will be difficult to handle, the steering awkward, and a capsize will seem too close for comfort. If you feel the wind getting too strong, go home at once before it is too late, particularly if there are no other boats near you. Beginners tend to underestimate the strength of the wind, particularly on a sunny day.

SAIL TRIM

Sail trimming is the essence of good sailing. It is a skill which develops with experience, but the development is greatly accelerated if the sailor is aware of the effects of poor trimming. When sailing with the wind forward of the beam, i.e. into the wind, the sheets must be pulled in so that the luff of each sail is just not 'lifting', that is, there is no sign of the sail fluttering. If the sail lifts its aerodynamic character is affected and you lose forward drive. If the sail is sheeted in too hard it will set badly, lose efficiency, produce unnecessary heeling tendency and unbalance the steering. The sheeting of the jib affects the mainsail for if it is sheeted in too hard it will backwind the mainsail causing it to lift near the mast and thus lose aerodynamic drive. As I said in Chapter 1, the sails are most efficient when set at about 22° to the wind. The best way to judge that you have the sheets just right is frequently to ease them a little until the luff of the sail starts to lift, then harden in again an inch or two. However, when beating into the wind, close-hauled, the sails are hauled in tight and instead of the sails being trimmed to the wind the whole boat is steered so that the sails are drawing properly and not lifting. Many people like to attach a small piece of wool to each side of the sail, a few inches back from the luff and about a third of the way up. When the sail is trimmed correctly both windward and leeward pieces of wool are blown smoothly back, indicating a smooth air flow. If your sails are sheeted too far in or out the pieces of wool will flutter about, showing that the air flow is turbulent.

When sailing with the wind abaft the beam you cannot judge the set of the sails by the lift of the luff. Instead you have to judge by the behaviour of the boat, its speed and heel, and set the sheets so that the boat is sailing quickly and easily. When the wind is so far aft that you are running let the mainsheet out so that the boom is against the leeward shrouds. The jib may not fill very well and it may be better to haul it out on the opposite side so that the boat is sailing 'goose-winged'. In light winds the clew of the jib may be supported by a jib stick, or whisker pole, (See Fig. 30) which is hooked on to the mast.

The fore-and-aft trim of the boat affects speed, by altering the area of the hull submerged, and steering, by altering the position of the centre of lateral resistance (see Chapter 1). It is usually about right if the transom is just on the water, but this is difficult to judge, except by asking another boat, as if you lean over to look you affect the trim!

Heeling is an important factor. Dinghies are designed to sail upright and excessive heel reduces speed in several ways. First, it increases the wetted surface of the hull. Second, the underwater shape of a hull when heeled over has an asymmetrical, less hydrodynamically efficient shape. Third, the effective area of the sails presented to the wind is smaller. Fourth, the effective area of the centreboard and rudder is less, so leeway may be greater. Fifth, it upsets the steering balance.

For these reasons you must always try to keep the boat sailing upright. This means that in a strong wind both crew and helmsman will have to lean right over the windward side, with their toes under the toestraps in the bottom of the boat to stop them falling out. High performance dinghies often have a trapeze, which is a wire from the mast which the crew clips to a harness worn round his bottom. He can then stand on the side of the boat leaning out backwards. A few boats have seats which move on a slide right out over the water. Both these devices mean that the crew can exert a greater force to keep the boat upright and the boat can therefore carry a larger area of sail.

If the combined weight of the crew will not hold the dinghy upright the inexperienced crew should let go of the mainsheet. The mainsheet is your safety valve: let it go in an emergency and the boat will slow down and the heeling force drop. But don't fall out of the boat backwards when she comes upright!

OBSTRUCTIONS

It is important to keep a good look-out for obstructions in the water. There are fixed objects such as buoys, rocks and moored boats, and moving objects such as driftwood, other boats, water skiers and swimmers. Except for other boats, you have to avoid these obstructions by changing course, tacking if necessary. In certain circumstances boats will avoid you, though you must always be ready to take evasive action if boats which should give way to you do not seem to have seen you or cannot or will not avoid you. A collision is always your fault as well as the other skipper's, except in a few special cases for racing boats.

The behaviour of boats meeting other boats is governed by the International Regulations for Preventing Collisions at Sea, often called the Rule of the Road. A completely new set of regulations came into force in July, 1977. While the content is not much changed the layout and numbering of rules is completely different to previous sets, so make sure that you do not study an old set. A booklet containing the new regulations can be purchased from the RYA.

The important rules for the dinghy sailor are as follows:

1. A boat which is overtaking another boat must keep clear of the boat which is being overtaken. This applies even when a sailing boat is overtaking a power boat.
2. In other circumstances a power-driven boat must give way to a sailing boat. (But in practice you must keep well clear of big ships as they are too unwieldy to give way to small boats.)
3. When sailing boats on opposite tacks meet, the one on the port tack must give way to the one on the starboard tack. (If it seems that the port tack boat is not going to take evasive action the starboard boat shouts 'starboard' very loudly, and prepares to alter course should it be necessary. Only a foolhardy skipper would risk collision on a matter of principle.)
4. When sailing boats on the same tack meet, the one which is to windward must keep out of the way of the one to leeward.

Boats which are racing are bound by the Rule of the Road when meeting boats which are not racing but it is courteous to keep well clear of them so that neither their wind nor their concentration is disturbed. Racing sailors will not hesitate to let you know if they think you are messing about with them. A racing dinghy will often carry a square burgee at the masthead; although this is no longer specified in the racing rules covering Britain many clubs still require it. A dinghy or yacht which is not racing carries a triangular burgee, if it carries one at all.

POSITION RELATIVE TO THE SHORE

Keep a good check on your position, and remember any known fixed hazards such as rocks, sandbanks or breakwaters. Do not get very far from your base in case conditions change or you have an accident or breakage and need to get back quickly. It is usually worth while getting to windward of it so that you have an easier sail if things get nasty, but if you are sailing in strong currents or tides in a light wind go up current so that it will carry you home. (But do not sail at all in strong currents unless there is enough wind for you to cover ground against the current or you never will get home.)

Make sure that the tide is not carrying you into danger, but remember that if disaster threatens you can often anchor while you work out the best solution or even just wait for the tide to turn.

RETURNING TO SHORE

The way in which you approach the shore depends on the direction of the wind relative to the shore. The various approaches are described in Chapter 6. When returning to shore keep a close watch on the depth of the water and raise the centreboard and rudder as soon as it becomes shallow. Do not wait for the centreboard to touch bottom as it may get damaged or jammed in the case as well as slowing the boat right down just as you need a little momentum to take it into yet shallower water and save you getting wet above the knees. Come ashore as gently as you can, and if you have to approach with a fresh or strong following wind make sure that you lower the main and come in under jib alone as you might damage the boat on the shore if you come in too fast. Step out just before the boat touches, then lower the sails and remove the rudder. Carry the boat out of the water or hold it floating while one of the crew gets the launching trolley. Never drag it out if you can avoid it; this can ruin the bottom surface. If the boat is beached, do make sure the rudder is removed before tipping the boat so that the trolley can be pushed under.

UNRIGGING

1. Lower the sails, making sure that you don't let go of the halyards. Cleat the halyards temporarily.
2. Take out the mainsail battens.
3. Undo the fittings attaching the mainsail to the boom ends.
4. Pull the mainsail gently off the mast and boom. Unshackle the head of the sail and stow the halyard by taking a loop through the shackle and over the cleat, then cleat the loose end, coiling the remains neatly.
5. Unshackle the head of the jib and stow the jib halyard. Unhank the jib from the forestay and detach the foot. Unreeve the jib

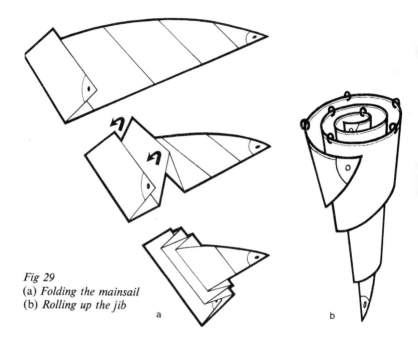

Fig 29
(a) *Folding the mainsail*
(b) *Rolling up the jib*

a   b

sheets from the fairleads.

6. Fold the sails neatly as shown in Fig. 29 and stow them in sailbags. Never fold the wire in the luff of the jib or you will make a kink which will spoil the set of the luff and risk breaking the strands of the wires. If the sails have transparent windows avoid folding these.

7. Remove the water from inside by removing drain plugs and using a sponge. If there are plugs in buoyancy compartments remove these to let them air. If any significant amount of water comes out the compartment has a leak which must be found and repaired.

8. Clean all dirt off the boat, not forgetting the inside of the centre-board case.

9. Stow the boom and mainsheet neatly. Stow the rudder inboard or take it away with any other moveable equipment such as oars, anchor, flare pack.

10. If there is time, let the boat dry before putting on the waterproof cover.

Chapter 6

Points of Sailing: Running, Reaching, Beating

Running

When the wind is dead aft of the boat or up to 25° either side, the boat is running before the wind. This is the easiest point of sailing to understand but is potentially hazardous because the boat can become unbalanced very quickly.

When running the sail is acting as a simple obstruction to the wind which pushes against it. There is no aerodynamic lifting effect and the sails are trimmed at right angles to the boat with the mainsheet right out and the main boom up against one of the shrouds. The jib is usually set 'goosewinged', extended on the opposite side to the mainsail, supported if necessary by a jib stick. Unless the wind is absolutely dead aft the mainsail should be set on the leeward side of the boat. This will reduce the likelihood of an involuntary gybe in which a shift in the wind direction or the helmsman allowing the boat to yaw off course lets the wind get the other side of the mainsail and slam the boom violently from one side of the boat to the other, sometimes butting the crew on the head en route and often causing a capsize.

As the force of the wind is almost completely behind the boat there is little tendency to heel and no tendency to be pushed off course, i.e. to make leeway. The centreboard can be lifted most of the way out of the water and the members of the crew can sit comfortably on either side of the boat presenting as large an area to the wind as they can so that they are like additional sails. However, because the mainsail has a much greater area than the jib the force of the wind is not directly over the centre line of the boat but to the side on which the mainsail is set and the boat will tend to luff. This tendency can, of course, be counteracted by the rudder but in light airs and with fairly smooth water it is

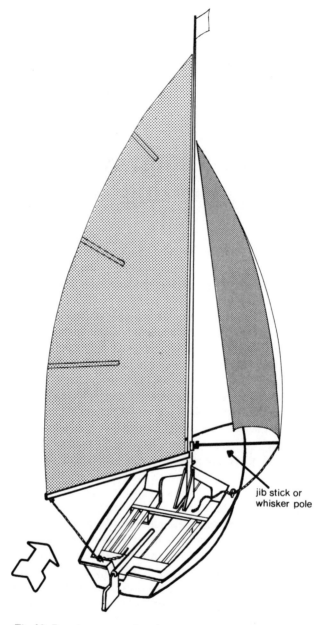

jib stick or
whisker pole

Fig 30 Running goose-winged

more efficient to heel the boat slightly to windward when the change in the underwater shape of the hull makes the boat tend to bear away and the centre of effort of the sails is more nearly over the centre line.

As the wind blows against the mainsail the sail has a tendency to fold up and twist, raising the boom high in the air. This not only reduces the area of sail presented to the wind but can also make steering difficult and increase the risk of a sudden gybe, so make sure the kicking strap is used.

In a strong wind the bows are inclined to dig into the water and the crew should move aft to avoid this. At all times the crew should sit as still as possible and move gently, as every movement will tend to make the boat roll. If the rolling becomes excessive it is a good idea to lower the centreboard further to damp down the motion.

It is difficult to control the speed of a boat on the run since this is determined by the force of the wind and the waterline length of the boat. Obviously the boat cannot go at the speed of the wind as there would then be no propulsive force but in a light wind the boat will go at 80% to 90% of the wind speed, i.e. in a 5 knot breeze a normal boat will reach 4 knots. As the wind rises the boat will reach its maximum hull speed. If the boat is inclined to plane on the run, go home, for the wind is too strong and the boat will be difficult to handle on the other points of sailing. The only way of stopping a boat on the run is to luff right up until the wind is forward of the beam.

GYBING

Changing course when on a run so that the wind is coming from the other side of the boat is called gybing. It is a manoeuvre which needs a great deal of care because there is drive from the wind all the time and the boat can easily become unbalanced.

When the helmsman decides that he is going to gybe he calls, "Ready to gybe". The crewman will then remove the jib stick, if it is in use, make certain that the jib sheets are free to run and then get hold of the boom or the kicking strap. The helmsman steers the boat round towards the new course. When the wind is dead aft he calls, "Gybe-oh" and moves over to the other side of the boat, ducking so that the boom will not hit him. At the same moment the crewman hauls on the boom to bring it over. When the wind catches the back of the sail it will blow over with a rush, tending to luff the boat, and the helmsman must counteract the luff. The crewman then tends the jib.

If the wind is strong and gybing with the boom right out means that

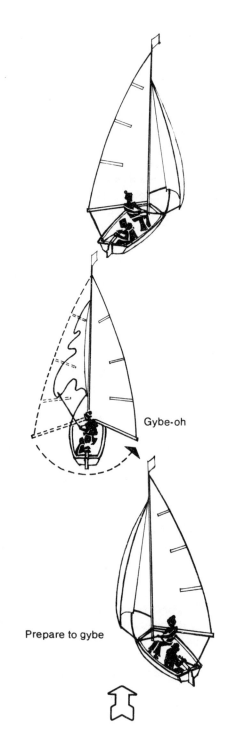

Gybe-oh

Prepare to gybe

Fig 31 Gybing

the boom will swing over with such force that a capsize is likely it is a good idea to sheet in the mainsail so that the sail is about half way in. The boat will now carry considerable weather helm, the boom has less distance to travel and the helmsman can take some of the force out of the gybe by letting the mainsheet run, checking it as the boom approaches the shrouds.

Reaching

If running is the most comfortable, albeit potentially hazardous, point of sailing, reaching is the most exciting. One can steer a course for one's destination, the boat attains its maximum speed and in a light boat there is always the possibility of an exhilarating, sizzling plane when the boat seems to be flying over the water in a welter of spray. If sailing consisted only of running and beating I suspect it would be a far less popular sport.

The sector of wind for reaching is large, and it is customary to distinguish between a close reach, a reach (or beam reach) and a broad reach, as shown in Chapter 2.

On a close reach the sails will be sheeted quite far in, and as the course becomes further off the wind the sheets will be let out. The sails work most effectively when the airflow over them is smooth. Once it becomes turbulent the aerodynamic thrust is lost and the boat will slow down. Wind tunnel tests show that for the maximum aerodynamic effect the sails should be set so that the wind strikes them at an angle of about 22°. This is borne out in practice.

When reaching it is important to understand the relationship between the true direction and strength of the wind, the boat's speed and direction and the apparent direction and strength of the wind. When a boat is underway its forward motion makes the wind appear to come from a different direction to that when the boat is stationary.

Suppose that there is no wind at all but a boat is moving forward under oars or engine, or indeed a water current. It will seem as though there is a wind blowing from in front of the boat at a strength equal to the boat's speed. This is the relative wind.

If there is a wind blowing as well it will combine with the relative wind to produce an apparent wind. If we draw lines whose lengths represent the speed of the boats (i.e. relative wind) and the true wind and their directions, and make a parallelogram with these lines as sides (this is known as a parallelogram of forces) the apparent wind will be represented by the diagonal of the parallelogram.

45

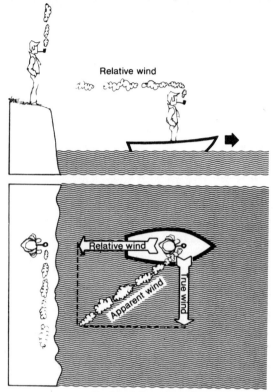

Fig 32 Relative wind

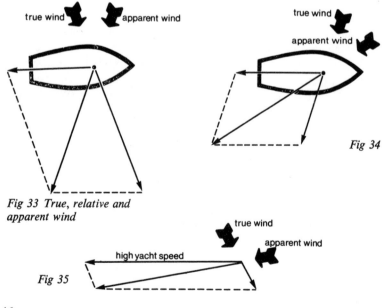

Fig 33 True, relative and apparent wind

Fig 34

Fig 35

From the sailing point of view it is the apparent wind which is important as this is what drives the sails. When the true wind is forward of the beam the apparent wind is stronger than the true wind and comes from further forward (Fig. 34). When the true wind is abaft the beam the apparent wind is less strong than the true wind but still seems to come from further forward. (Fig. 35.) The difference in direction between true and apparent wind is greatest when reaching. If the true wind is constant in direction but the boat speed increases (perhaps you have trimmed the sails) the apparent wind will increase in strength and move forward in direction. It is a curious thing that ice yachts which have so little resistance to motion sail close hauled to the apparent wind even if the true wind is aft because the boat speed is the dominant component of the parallelogram of forces (Fig. 36).

SAIL AND BOAT TRIM ON A CLOSE AND BEAM REACH

Except on a broad reach the flow of air over the sails is smooth and the sails are acting as aerofoils, providing 'lift'. As we said earlier (Chapter 1) the drive produced by the sail acts at right angles to it. Just as we drew a parallelogram of forces to show the apparent wind so we can draw a parallelogram of forces to discover the forces acting on the direction the boat is going and sideways to it. Fig. 37 shows that as the boat sails further off the wind so more of the force is acting to propel

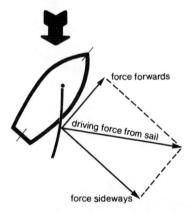

Fig 36 Sailing close-hauled even when the wind is aft

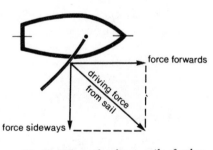

Fig 37 When the boat sails further off the wind the sideways force decreases relative to the forward force

the boat forward and less is trying to push it sideways. This is why the boat goes fastest when approximately on a beam reach. Because the sideways force is decreasing you will need less centreboard down as the reach gets broader.

To get the best airflow and drive from the sails, sheet them so that they are smooth and quiet. Since the sails interact with one another it is difficult to judge exactly the right position, but as a guide they should be set so that the jib is just not lifting and similarly the mainsail is smooth with no backwinding from the jib. Play with the sheets so that you feel you are getting maximum drive from the sails, remembering that the direction and strength of the apparent wind will be continually changing as the true wind fluctuates and your boat's speed varies. Remember that sails are most efficient when set at an angle of about 22° to the apparent wind, as indicated by the burgee. Many people put on thread a few inches back from the luff of each sail so that they have a delicate indication of whether the air flow is smooth.

The fore-and-aft trim of the boat should be normal (i.e. similar to the rest position) unless the speed is so high that there is a chance of planing when a shift aft may lift the boat on to a plane, inducing a sudden, exciting, increase in speed. If it doesn't get the boat planing go back to normal. If the boat starts to plane and you want to stop it, move your weight forward.

Always be prepared for changes in heeling tendency when you sit out. If the wind strength suddenly drops or the direction changes and the sails stall you will have to get back into the boat pretty quickly. Alternatively you can luff up to increase the heeling force, but you need to do it smartly.

Keep as still as you can in the boat so that you don't upset the airflow and the boat trim, particularly when planing.

If you want to slow down, ease the sheets.

A close reach is a wet part of sailing so, if you haven't got self bailers, bail out whenever you have a chance.

THE BROAD REACH

As the wind comes from further aft on a reach there eventually comes a point when you cannot set the sails at an angle to the wind which allows the air to flow smoothly over the sails. Abruptly the sail 'stalls' and the air flow becomes turbulent, as when running. The propulsive force immediately drops, as does the boat speed. This stalling point is quite precise and for a Bermuda sail is about 30° or a bit less and it means that you can sail a course almost the same as another boat but with quite a different speed: one boat will have smooth flow and good drive, the other will have turbulent flow and poor drive. To regain smooth flow you must luff up quite a lot to get up speed which will increase the strength of the wind and bring it further ahead, then you can bear away toward the stalling point.

A broad reach is similar in many ways to a run except that it is less dangerous since the chance of an involuntary gybe is much less.

Beating

Beating, or sailing close hauled, means sailing into the wind as much as possible. The course taken by the boat is dictated by the wind and not by the destination the helmsman wishes to reach. Because a dinghy can only sail at about 45° to the wind it is necessary to take a zig-zag course to a destination which is more or less directly to windward. Each zig or zag is known as a tack or, more correctly but less frequently, a board.

Other things being equal, there is no difference in the distance you have to sail between making a lot of short tacks or a few long ones. Other things, however, are seldom equal. There may be fixed obstructions in the water or other boats likely to interfere, and the quality and quantity of wind and current may well differ in different places. The helmsman must therefore judge the right length of tack and the right place at which to put about on to a new tack. In general, it is inefficient to make a large number of short tacks as an inordinate amount of time is lost in putting the boat about and regaining speed on the new course. It is equally unadvisable to make very long tacks as you risk being caught by an unfavourable change in the wind as well as the likelihood of misjudging the right moment to put about.

When sailing close hauled to windward the helmsman is always making a compromise between pointing the boat as high as possible, to reduce the distance he must sail, and keeping the speed of the boat high.

There are a lot of factors which influence the effectiveness of the close-hauled boat. These are sail trim, weight distribution, speed and smoothness in putting about (tacking) and the way in which the boat is handled in variable winds. A dirty or rough bottom of the boat will reduce the forward speed.

When sailing close hauled one must always appreciate that the direction in which the boat is actually going is not the same as the direction in which it is pointed because there is always a strong sideways force

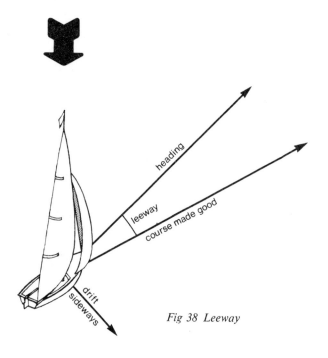

Fig 38 Leeway

in addition to the forward propulsive force. The angle between the boat's heading and the course made good is known as the leeway, e.g. one could say 'the boat is making about five degrees of leeway'. (Fig. 38) The amount of leeway made depends mainly on the forward speed of the boat as the sideways force does not vary very much.

There is an inverse relationship between heading and speed: the closer to the wind the boat points the lower will be the speed, partly because the sails actually produce less drive and partly because what drive is produced is acting at a more acute angle. Because the speed is low, the leeway will be high. When the boat's heading is further off the wind the speed goes up and the leeway goes down. A change in heading of only a degree or two can increase the speed quite considerably, because the sails can act more efficiently, while the distance to be sailed is only increased a little bit. Beginners are inclined to point the boat too high, understandably feeling that if the boat is pointing high the course made good will be better. When sailing close-hauled the wind would blow the boat right over sideways if the crew did not prevent it because the sideways force is so great. In anything of a wind both members of the crew must lean right out over the windward side to prevent a capsize and in many racing dinghies the crewman will suspend himself by a 'trapeze' wire from the mast so that he can stand on the edge of the boat and lean right out so that his weight is much more effective. The way of using a trapeze is described in Chapter 7.

SAIL AND BOAT TRIM FOR BEATING

It is particularly important when sailing to windward to have a really taut luff on the jib. If the luff is slack the sail balloons out and the leach tends to curve back to windward, directing the drive from the sail more across the boat reducing the forward propulsive component of the wind force.

To get the jib to set properly it is also important that the jib sheets are led at the right angle from the sail to the boat. If your boat has jib fairleads whose position can be adjusted, fix them at the point which makes the luff of the sail start to shake down its whole length at the same time or perhaps slightly earlier at the top. If it starts to shake at the top long before it shakes at the bottom, the jib fairlead is too far aft. Conversely, if it starts to shake first at the bottom the jib fairlead is too far forward.

Similarly the mainsail needs adjustment so that the wind will flow smoothly over it. In a strong wind it should be set flat by stretching the foot well out on the boom and having the boom down hard. In a light wind the sail should be set fuller, reducing the tension on the bolt ropes by not having the foot and luff so tight. If the lead of the mainsheet is adjustable it should be positioned so that the sail is not twisted.

The sails should be sheeted in fairly hard and kept drawing by altering course as the apparent wind fluctuates in direction. If you have threads of wool or cotton through the luff of the sails you will be able to see quite clearly when the wind flow becomes turbulent. If you pinch the boat too close to the wind so that your boat speed drops, bear away to pick up speed and then luff up gently until the flow over the sail is still just smooth.

When the true wind increases in strength the apparent wind also increases in strength and comes from slightly further aft. It is therefore a good idea to luff up in the gusts both to make a better course to windward and to reduce the extra heeling force applied by the stronger wind. However, luffing in the gusts calls for discretion as too large a luff will stall the sails which may even be caught aback. Beginners should practise this technique, but should always be ready to let fly the mainsheet as a safety measure.

The boat should be sailed upright or at a very slight angle of heel. As the heeling force varies the crew must alter their positions to counteract it. If a sudden gust of wind strikes and the helmsman is not able to take the sting out of it by luffing he can easily reduce the heeling force by letting out the mainsheet which will immediately reduce both the forward and sideways force. Letting out the mainsheet is the helmsman's safety device, which will slow the boat rapidly and reduce the heel dramatically if anything goes wrong: for example, if the crewman slips and falls into the boat, or indeed, if he slips and falls out of the boat! However, it is tiring to be continually hauling the mainsheet tight again so it is advantageous to develop the technique of luffing in the gusts.

When sailing at sea quite long waves may be encountered, and for two reasons these can affect the apparent wind. The first reason is that the boat is actually sailing up and downhill, slowly as she goes up, which will bring the apparent wind aft, and speeding up as she goes down, which will bring the apparent wind forward and stronger. In addition the water is actually moving forward at the crest and back in the trough. Therefore, for really efficient sailing it pays to luff at the top of the waves, as though one were luffing in a gust, and bear away in the troughs.

TACKING (PUTTING ABOUT, GOING ABOUT)

This is the manoeuvre in which you change from one tack to the other. When done properly it takes place smoothly, quickly and with little fuss, but this depends on timing and co-ordination between the members of the crew.

When the helmsman decides that he is going to tack he calls 'Ready About'. The crewman then makes sure that the jib sheets are ready to run freely and if the jib is in a jam cleat he uncleats it and takes the strain himself. The helmsman moves the tiller away from his body to leeward and calls "lee-oh". The tiller must be moved gently but firmly for if it is moved too abruptly it will act as a brake. As the boat heads into the wind the jib will begin to flap. The crew should not slacken the jib sheet until the jib has stopped pulling. When it lifts he lets go of the sheet and hauls in on the opposite one, making certain that he does not sheet in the jib until it starts to fill on the new tack. If he is too quick he may sheet it in aback and stop the boat head to wind, 'in stays' as it is known. It is then difficult to start sailing again. On the other hand he may be too late, in which case not only will it lose drive but in a fresh breeze it will be very difficult to haul it in tight.

While this is happening both members of the crew move to the opposite side of the boat and the helmsman steers to the new course, being careful not to let the boat bear away too far.

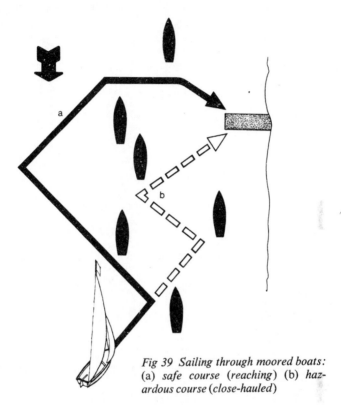

Fig 39 Sailing through moored boats: (a) *safe course* (*reaching*) (b) *hazardous course* (*close-hauled*)

OBSTRUCTIONS

When sailing close-hauled the boat is restricted in its manoeuvrability, so when sailing near obstructions it is necessary to take care to choose a course which will not lead into trouble. The problems are:
1. You can't luff much without stopping, so to clear an obstruction you may need to go about, which needs room.
2. Although it is easy to slow down it is difficult to speed up except by bearing away.
3. If the wind heads you, you must bear away.

4. If going about is difficult because of the wind and sea conditions you must allow room to try again, or to lower sail and gybe.

For these reasons it is a good idea to work well up to windward of difficult obstructions like moored boats and to negotiate them on a reach. Always pass to leeward of an obstruction: if you pass close to windward and for any reason your speed drops you may well find yourself blown into it.

Chapter 7

Trapezing and Spinnaker Handling

The trapeze is a comparatively recent piece of equipment for increasing the speed at which a boat can go. It enables the crewman to use his weight more effectively to counteract the heeling tendency of a dinghy so that a larger sail area can be carried.

The trapeze consists of two parts: two wires, one suspended each side from the mast, and a harness which the crewman wears and which can be attached to the wire. The crewman is then able to lean right out over the water with his feet on the gunwale and his weight supported by the mast. It sounds rather gymnastic but is in fact less strain on the muscles than the usual sitting out position. The wire from the mast has a special ring of some kind for attachment on to the harness and this has a grip handle for the crew to hold. The harness is usually made of canvas and fits snugly over the crew's bottom and between his legs and has a metal plate with a hook or other attachment for the wire. Often shoulder straps are worn to keep the harness in place. It is important that the harness should be adjustable so that it can be made to fit well and that it should be well padded over the hips and small of the back.

The trapeze must be used as soon as the boat cannot be kept upright just by sitting out with toestraps. To get out the crew holds the jib sheet in his aft hand, gets hold of the trapeze wire with his forward hand and hooks it on to his harness. Then, with his aft foot still under the toestrap he brings his forward foot on to the gunwale so that it presses against the shroud attachment. He grabs the grip handle on the wire and pushes outward using only his forward leg. Because the

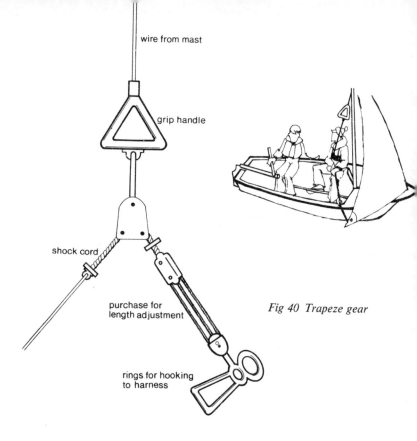

wire from mast

grip handle

shock cord

purchase for
length adjustment

Fig 40 Trapeze gear

rings for hooking
to harness

trapeze wire is attached to the boat forward of the crew it will try to pull him towards the bows so he uses his forward leg to counteract this pull. As he pushes himself out his aft hand lengthens the jib sheet and as soon as he is out he lets go of the grip handle with his forward hand and takes over the jib sheet.

To get in again, he takes the sheet in his aft hand, and the grip handle in his forward hand. Then he takes his aft foot off the gunwale and, by bending his forward knee, eases himself into a sitting position. However, if the dinghy is about to tack he must bend his aft leg and find a foothold in the cockpit with his forward leg. He then unhooks himself from the wire, makes a half turn facing aft under the kicking strap as the boat tacks, attaches himself to the other wire and gets out on the new windward side. If the trapeze is used for reaching as well as beating the crew will need to be further aft (for planing). The trapeze wire will have two rings to allow for the two positions.

The length of the wire must be such that the crew is suspended at right-angles to the mast, and the length will therefore depend on how

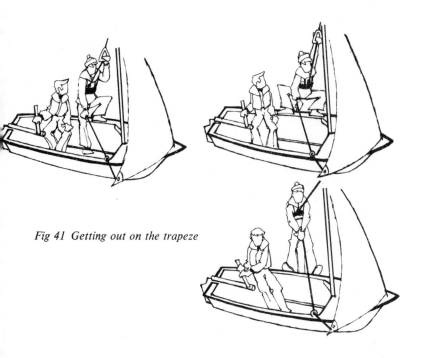

Fig 41 Getting out on the trapeze

tall the crewman is. There must always be a quick method of detaching the harness in case of a capsize.

Because it is tiring for the crew to be continually getting in and out on the trapeze the helmsman must do all he can to keep his crew out, even to the extent of moving momentarily to leeward. He must be careful not to luff too suddenly and make the boat heel to windward, ducking the trapeze man. The helmsman cannot let the mainsheet run in an emergency as the boat will capsize to windward on top of the crew. On a reach the helmsman must haul in the mainsheet quickly when the wind drops so that the heeling force is sufficient to support the trapeze man.

SPINNAKER HANDLING

The spinnaker is a very full headsail which is shaped roughly like part of a sphere and is attached to the boat only by its corners. Some spinnakers, particularly on ocean racing yachts, are enormous, others

57

are much smaller but it is not worth using a spinnaker on any boat unless its area is at least equal to that of the jib and mainsail together. Because it is only attached to the boat by its three corners it must be kept properly trimmed or it will collapse and lose its pull. However, it is a conventional sail with a leech, a luff and a foot, a head, a tack and a clew. It is different in that when the course is changed so that the wind is coming from the other side of the boat the previous luff becomes the new leach, the previous tack becomes the new clew. The bottom corners of the sail are attached to the boat by ropes, the one leading to the tack (the windward corner) being called the guy, the one leading to the clew (the leeward corner) being called the sheet. The tack of the sail is supported by a spinnaker boom, a pole which is pivoted at the mast, and held in position by the topping lift and downhaul which are hooked on to the middle of the boom.

The reasons why spinnaker handling can be confusing to the novice and rather more prone to accident even for the expert are (i) the spinnaker is hoisted while sailing (ii) the sail must be kept full of air or it will collapse and may get twisted (iii) it is difficult for the novice to remember which is tack and clew, sheet and guy.

Before the spinnaker is hoisted it must be carefully stowed in a bag, net bucket or chute so that the head appears first, ready to be clipped on to the spinnaker halyard, the two corners following with their lines attached (frequently a red line to the port corner and a green line to the starboard corner). The rest of the sail must be stowed without any twisting so that it will hoist smoothly, ready to fill.

The steps the crew takes hoisting and setting the spinnaker are as follows:
1. Attach spinnaker halyard to sail.
2. Pass the sheets round all the rigging (shrouds and stays) and rig through the fairleads at the stern.
3. Give the sheet and guy to the helmsman. While the helmsman hoists the spinnaker, guide it so that the head does not get caught in anything.
4. Clip one end of the spinnaker boom to the tack.
5. Attach the topping lift and downhaul (which are joined together) to their fitting in the middle of the boom.
6. Clip the other end of the pole to the mast while the helmsman puts out the guy.
7. Take the sheet and guy from the helmsman and trim the sail.

To trim the sail correctly, first haul in the guy until the luff begins to shake, then adjust the sheet so that the leech is just on the point of

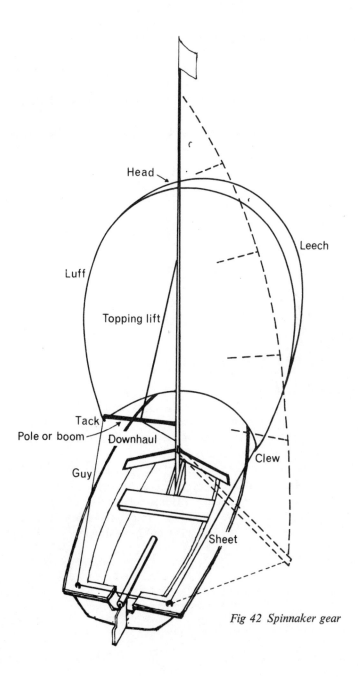

Head

Leech

Luff

Topping lift

Tack

Pole or boom

Downhaul

Guy

Clew

Sheet

Fig 42 Spinnaker gear

59

lifting. Once this is done the guy is cleated and the sheet used for small adjustments.

In light winds the helmsman sits to leeward while the crew sits to windward, watching the luff of the sail all the time and continually playing the sheet. In a fresher wind both members of the crew sit inboard to minimize rolling. If there are strong puffs of wind you can ease the sheet to spill wind and in an emergency let it fly. If by mischance the guy is let fly the spinnaker boom will swing forward until it strikes the forestay. The sail is now pulling sideways and will likely enough capsize the boat.

To gybe the spinnaker:
1. The helmsman gybes the mainsail first.
2. The crew unclips the spinnaker boom from the mast. The helmsman eases the sheet and guy, which now change names—the old sheet is the new guy, the old guy is the new sheet.
3. The crew clips the fore end of the boom on to it, new tack (old clew), unclips the other end from the old tack and clips it on to the mast.
4. The crew trims the spinnaker with sheet and guy as before.

To lower the spinnaker:
1. Pay out both sheet and guy until the sail collapses.
2. Detach the pole from the mast, take off the topping lift and downhaul and unclip it from the tack.
3. Keep hold of the tack and pull in the clew to join it.
4. Let the halyard go, and feed the sail into its container as it drops. Don't let it fall into the water or the boat may sail over it and get it fouled round centreboard and rudder.

Many boats now have a spinnaker chute. This is a chute in the bows of the boat. A retrieving line is attached to the centre of the spinnaker and led through the chute. When this line is hauled in the spinnaker is pulled neatly down the chute and is ready to be used again. A retrieving line makes it much easier to lower the sail in fresh winds.

Chapter 8

Seamanship

Seamanship is the art of doing the right thing at the right time when dealing with boats and water. It is something which develops with experience and is what distinguishes a good sailor from a bad one. The good sailor will be able to size up a situation and approach it in a safe and effective manner so that he achieves his aim with the minimum of fuss and bother. However, despite the need for experience, there are a number of basic procedures which every sailor should learn. It is a good idea to practise all these procedures, including capsizing, under safe conditions so that when they have to be performed in danger you have the experience and confidence to do what needs to be done without fuss or panic.

SAILING UNDER JIB ALONE

Sailing under jib alone is a skill well worth practising as it is necessary for carrying out many of the manoeuvres described in this chapter.

It is not possible to sail very close to the wind under jib alone because the centre of effort is forward of the centre of lateral resistance so it swings the boat away from the wind and because the speed will be lower, because the sail area is smaller, so leeway will be greater. However, sailing under the jib alone is usually used when undertaking a manoeuvre with a fresh wind aft so that the boat's speed is less, so lack of ability to sail well to windward is not critical.

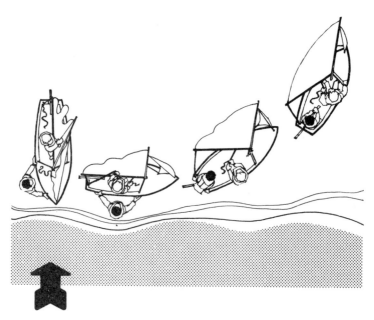

Fig 43 *Leaving a windward shore*

Fig 44 *Leaving with the wind along the shore*

62

To get as close to the wind as possible, about 70°, put the centreboard down and sheet the jib so that it is just not lifting at the luff. Heel the boat over a bit so that it has a tendency to turn into the wind. To go about under jib alone is difficult and if you have enough room it is simpler to gybe. If you have to tack get up as much speed as possible, then slowly put the tiller to leeward and heel the boat to leeward. As you come up into the wind sheet the jib progressively harder until it is flat. As soon as the boat is head to wind back the jib by holding the clew to windward. Make sure the boat is right round on the new tack before sheeting the jib on the new side.

LEAVING A BEACH

The way in which you leave a beach or slipway depends on the direction and strength of the wind. It is quite simple when wind is astern or abeam but more difficult when the wind is ahead.

When the wind is astern put the boat in the water stern first so that it is head to wind. The crew gets aboard and lowers the centreboard and rudder a little. The helmsman then pivots the boat around until it is stern to wind, climbs in smartly and sails her off lowering rudder and centreboard as soon as the water is deep enough.

The procedure with the wind abeam is similar. The helmsman again holds the boat head to wind while the crew climbs in and lowers the centreboard and rudder a little. The helmsman turns the boat across the wind and the crew sheets in the jib. The helmsman then pushes off and climbs in, taking the mainsheet and sheeting it in. Rudder and centreboard are lowered when possible.

Leaving a beach with an onshore wind is most difficult as the boat must pick up speed fast enough to avoid being blown back ashore. It is not uncommon to make several attempts in a strong wind particularly if there are sizeable waves as well. If you can find a slight kink in the shoreline which will allow you to leave on a close reach it will be easier. Unless the wind is exactly at right angles to the shore, choose the tack which will give you a better angle away from the shore, and choose the windward end of beach so that you have more room to get going.

The boat is placed in the water, bows first, and the helmsman holds it standing alongside the mast. The crew gets in and the helmsman wades forward with the boat. The crew lowers the centreboard and rudder a little and sheets in the jib. The helmsman gives a good shove, then jumps in. The boat will tend to bear away and the helmsman sheets in the main a bit. He steers a course almost parallel to the beach

to pick up speed, edging into deeper water, and when it is deep enough the crew lowers the centreboard and the helmsman gradually alters course to windward. It is important to keep the boat's speed up so that you can work gradually away from the shore. If you point too close to the wind the boat will lose forward speed and drift sideways back to the shore.

RETURNING TO THE BEACH

This is usually easier than leaving the beach except when there is a strong onshore wind. It is important to remember to lift the centreboard and rudder just before the boat beaches so that they are not damaged and the boat is not brought to a halt in unnecessarily deep water. If the centreboard is down anyone jumping overboard to beach the boat will get very wet. As soon as the boat beaches the crew jump out and carry it out of the water so that it is not damaged by the waves.

When the wind is off the shore you must approach with a number of tacks and when the water is too shallow for the centreboard, get up speed on a beam reach, then luff up and beach.

With a strong onshore wind it may be a good idea to sail in on a reach using only the jib, letting the mainsail flap, or even to lower the mainsail.

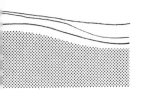

Fig 45 Leaving a lee shore

Fig 46 Approaching a lee shore

65

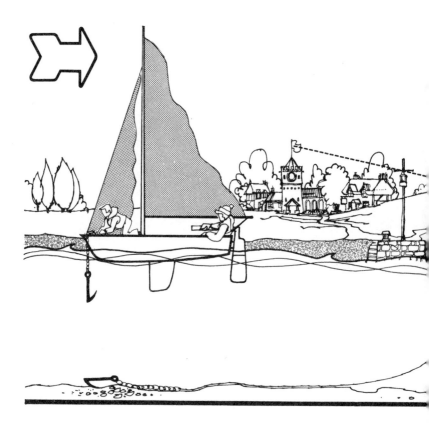

ANCHORING

Before anchoring check that the anchor is properly attached to the anchor rope and, equally important and sometimes forgotten, that the anchor rope is properly attached to the dinghy. Estimate the depth of water you are going to anchor in and measure out roughly four times that amount of rope. Make the rope fast at that point to the mooring cleat or round the mast and coil it so that it will run out without tangling.

When anchored the boat will lie head to wind astern of the anchor except in a light wind and strong current. You should therefore come head to wind and start going backwards before dropping the anchor so that it bites in the right direction. When the boat is making sternway the helmsman says 'Drop the anchor' and the crew drops the anchor alone over the bows. The rope will run out by itself but if you drop rope

Fig 47 Anchoring

and anchor over the side they are almost certain to get knotted up. When the anchor is all out drop the jib and raise the centreboard. Then check that the anchor is holding by taking two points in a line on the land. If they stay in a line the anchor is holding. If they separate the anchor is dragging and you must weigh it (haul it in) and try again.

WEIGHING ANCHOR

Hoist the sails, slip the rudder but leave the centreboard up. The crew hauls the anchor rope into the boat until it is vertical in the water. The helmsman decides which tack to leave on, the crew backs the jib and when the boat is pointing in the right direction he hands the jib sheet to the helmsman and 'breaks out' the anchor, hauling it aboard as fast as he can, then drops the centreboard.

If the helmsman and crew are used to working together it is possible to sail up to the anchor and break it out while in motion.

Picking up a mooring involves coming head to wind at the right moment so that the boat is stationary as the mooring buoy comes alongside the shrouds. You must know how much way your boat will carry—normally not much in a dinghy unless it is heavily built.

If it can be done, approach the mooring on a close reach. The helmsman takes charge of the jib sheet and the crew leans forward of the shroud ready to lift the mooring buoy rope into the dinghy, passing the rope between the forestay and the windward shroud. At the moment he judges right the helmsman luffs and lets the sheets fly. The crew picks up the mooring rope and passes it through the bow fairlead if there is one and takes a turn round the mooring cleat, if there is one, or round the mast. The sails are then quickly lowered and the mooring then made properly secure, lashing the mooring rope to the forestay if there is no bow fairlead. It is important to be sure that the boat is head to wind and that the crewman picks up the mooring rope near the bows or the boat may continue sailing and you may have to drop the mooring and make a new approach. To prevent the boat sheering about when it is moored, raise the centreboard and unship the rudder. If you are going to leave the boat on the mooring lift the buoy into the boat and secure direct to the mooring chain, unless it is too heavy for the boat to support. In this case use your anchor rope to make fast to the top of the chain and leave the buoy afloat. You make fast directly to the chain because the buoy and its rope are really only designed to float the chain and help you make fast; the chain is supposed to take the strain.

If there is a current or tide running you will be able to see how it affects the boats already moored. It may be worth making a dummy run so that you can find how fast it is running and when to luff.

LEAVING A MOORING

When both wind and current are in the same direction it is easy to leave a mooring. Rig the boat and slip the rudder. Decide which tack you are going to leave on. The crew prepares to let go the mooring, holding the chain and putting the buoy and buoy-rope over the side, forward of the shroud. The boat will swing round and the sails fill. As they fill the crew lets go the chain, the sheets are hauled in and the centreboard is lowered.

If the wind and current are in opposite directions the unrigged dinghy will be head to current. In anything of a breeze she will turn head to wind as soon as the sails are hoisted. In a light wind you take the mooring to the stern so that the boat has head to wind and leave as before.

Fig 48 Coming alongside a moored boat

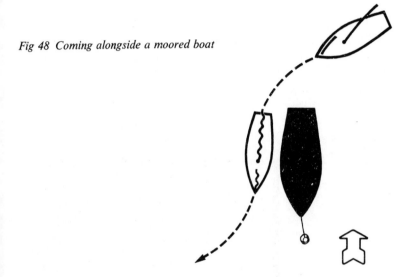

COMING ALONGSIDE A MOORED BOAT

The direction in which a moored boat is facing will be affected by both wind and current. If the current is weak the moored boat will lie head to wind and you can approach it in a similar way to a mooring, approaching on a close reach and luffing to arrive alongside with no forward motion. It is best to approach so that your windward side meets the other boat's side so that your main boom does not hit the other boat as you approach, and so that you can continue sailing if you have muffed the approach.

If the current is strong so that the moored boat is not head to wind, or the boat is moored fore-and-aft, approach it like a jetty (next section).

If there is a sea running and the other boat is large and heavy do not go alongside unless you have to as you are quite likely to get both your hands and your boat damaged.

69

The approach to a jetty, quayside or pontoon depends upon the direction of the wind relative to the jetty.

If the wind is along the jetty come up on the appropriate tack, luff up and grab hold.

If there is a wind blowing on to the jetty, come up with the wind on your beam, let the sheets fly and the wind will blow you sideways on to the jetty. If the jetty is higher than the boom, drop the mainsail first and come in under jib only.

If the position of the jetty means that you must approach with the wind aft drop the mainsail and come in under jib alone, or you will not be able to stop.

Sometimes, if the jetty or quay is very high and the wind is blowing off it there may be a calm in its lee. If your boat will not carry enough way to reach the jetty you may have to row or paddle the last few feet.

Fig 49 Approaching a jetty

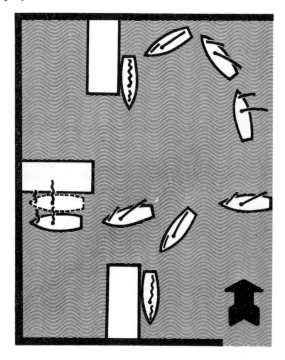

Capsizing is an unpleasant experience but it need not be frightening if you know how to recover from it. A capsize usually happens in a fairly strong breeze because of negligence, a mistake in judgement or broken equipment. Occasionally it happens because an exceptionally strong gust of wind arrives suddenly and sometimes one sees the amazing sight of a whole fleet of racing dinghies capsizing together.

The first and most important rule on a capsize is **hang on to the boat.** Do not try to swim ashore and do not go after pieces of equipment which are floating away. A boat is visible to a searcher when a swimmer is not.

Righting a capsized boat is an operation which may be very easy or very difficult depending on the boat, the sea conditions and the physical ability of the crew. A really experienced dinghy sailor can capsize and right the dinghy without getting his feet wet but usually the crew will find themselves in the water before they have had time to react.

A boat can capsize both to windward and to leeward. A windward capsize usually occurs when the crew are leaning right out to counteract a strong heeling force and there is a sudden lull in the wind which they are too slow to allow for. A leeward capsize is more common and occurs when a strong gust heels the boat over too far before the crew can counteract it. It will also happen if the crew slips into or out of the boat when beating.

If the boat capsizes on to its side it should be possible to right it. First, turn it head to wind and let one person hold it in that position. The other person climbs on to the centreboard, holds on to the gunwale and pulls the boat upright, climbing into it if he can. He then bails out as much water as possible while the other person moves to the stern and climbs in, using a loop in the mainsheet as a foothold if necessary. He must not try to climb in over the side or the boat will capsize again. If the boat cannot be righted with the sails hoisted because of their drag in the water take them off the boat, leaving the halyard attached so they do no float away.

If you still cannot right the boat you need help. If you are sailing in a race there will be a rescue boat present. If you are out by yourself you must make signals to attract attention to your plight. Repeatedly raising and lowering the outstretched arms or waving an article of clothing are recognized distress signals, as is a red flare or orange smoke signal. But even if no one appears to see you **stay with the boat until you are rescued.**

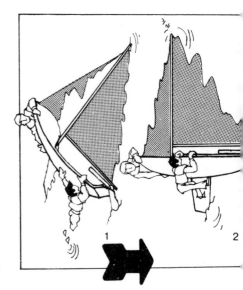

Fig 50 Righting a capsized boat

If the boat capsizes so that it is upside down it may be difficult to right it as the centreboard is likely to be out of reach. It might be possible to get a rope, say the jib sheet, over the hull from the other side and haul on that to bring the boat on to her side. If the bottom is shallow, the mast may stick in to it and be damaged or break. You will probably need help to free it.

Unless you are going to drift into trouble do not anchor a capsized boat as loose equipment will float quickly away and the swimming crew may become exhausted by the pull of the current.

Towing

There may be occasions when you need to tow or be towed by another boat. It is not quite as simple as it may appear and there are a few points to take into account.

WHEN YOU ARE BEING TOWED

Use the anchor rope as a tow rope, pass it through the bow fairlead if you have one, and secure it to a mooring cleat or the mast. Drop the sails and raise the centreboard. Trim the boat down by the stern and steer to follow the towing boat.

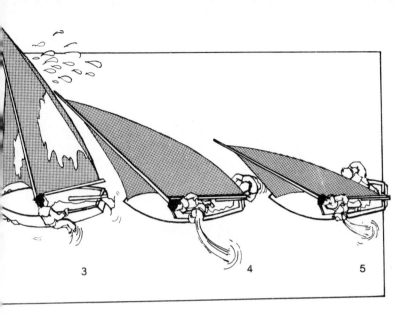

3   4   5

WHEN YOU ARE TOWING

Take the tow rope aboard and make it fast amidships, not at the stern where the pull will stop the rudder swinging the stern round to change course. If you are towing under sail and need to tack you must take the drag of the towed boat off your boat. Pull in about five metres of the tow rope, then get up speed by bearing away a little. Then go about and at the same time let out the rope, braking the last few feet by hand so that there is not a sudden jerk when it takes the strain again.

Chapter 9

Wind and Current

A basic knowledge of the way in which air and water flow and how the flow is affected by obstructions is a great help to a sailor in choosing a course that will not be unnecessarily difficult to sail. It is, however, practically impossible to work out exactly what conditions will be like just from looking at the configuration of land and buildings and it is worth picking the brains of people with local knowledge. Even so, make your own judgements, for it is well known that experts are not always right.

Because water behaves more predictably than wind I will describe its behaviour first, starting with steady continuous currents and then looking at tidal flows. In all the drawings the larger the arrow the faster the current.

Currents

STRAIGHT FLOW

The simplest situation is where water is flowing between straight and parallel banks. You might expect that the water would flow at the same speed all the way across but it does not. Because of the friction between the water and the banks it flows faster in the middle and more slowly at the sides. Because it flows faster in the middle the water tends to scour out a deeper channel which further increases the speed of the water in the middle.

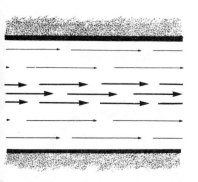

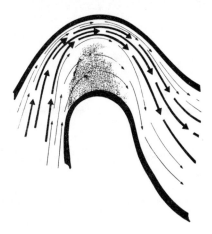

Fig 51 Water flowing in a straight channel

Fig 52 Water flowing round a bend

BENDS

When water flows round a bend it tries to keep going straight on. It therefore flows fastest on the outside of the bend and slowest on the inside. Because of the gentler flow inside silt is deposited to a greater or lesser extent forming a shallow bank so be careful not to go aground when sailing on the inside of a bend against the current. Sailing with the current you would go round the outside where the bank will be steep and cut away.

OBSTRUCTIONS

When there is an obstruction, such as an island, in mid-stream the water will flow round it forming, in effect, two narrower rivers. The current will diverge a small way upstream leaving a patch of slower water immediately ahead of the island and there will be a patch of slow water with some eddies below the island. The current will be speeded up in the two channels because there is less room for the water unless

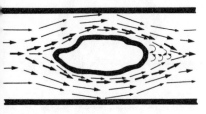

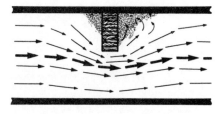

Fig 53 Water flowing round an obstruction

Fig 54 Water flowing round a jetty

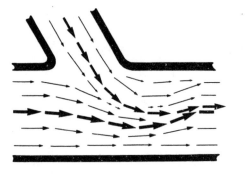

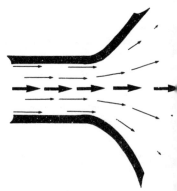

Fig 55 Secondary flow joining a greater flow

Fig 56 Water spreading from a ri mouth

the banks spread out. Submerged sandbanks give a similar but less marked effect.

If there is an obstruction sticking out from the bank like a jetty the water will be diverted round it, speeding up because the channel is briefly narrower and giving slack water above and below it with silt accumulating round its base.

SECONDARY FLOW

When another, smaller, river joins the first there will be a permanent increase in the amount of water flowing downstream and the current will therefore be greater. The main flow of water will be diverted by the pressure of the new flow joining it.

Fig 57 Back eddies formed in a small bay

RIVER MOUTH

Where a river flows into a lake or the sea the flow will spread out in a fan and be slower.

BAY CURRENTS

Where there are small bays in the banks of a river they are often filled with useful eddies.

TIDES

In the previous description of moving water the flow might have been due either to the current in a river or a tidal stream. The difference is that the former is steady in direction and changes speed only slowly whereas tidal streams are continually changing in both speed and direction.

Tidal streams are caused by the gravitational pull of the moon and, to a lesser extent, of the sun on the enormous mass of water in the earth's oceans. Because the water can flow it bulges out towards the moon with an equal bulge away from the moon. As the earth goes round the bulges move round the earth to keep in line with the moon and so twice a day a bulge passes over any place in the oceans.

Fig 58 The Moon pulls the Earth's envelope of water into a bulge

However, the moon is revolving round the earth once every four weeks and so there are not exactly 12 hours between successive high tides. The difference is actually 12 hours 26 minutes, so the difference between the time of high water on successive days is 52 minutes.

High water is when the tide is highest. It is followed by ebb during which the water recedes for about six hours. This is followed by low water, which is followed by flood. At high and low water the water level may remain the same for some period of time, known as stand of tide. The tidal flow ceases, giving slack water.

The cycle from high water, through ebb, low water and flood back to high water is known as the tidal cycle. During this cycle the rate at which the water flows varies. It is zero at high water, then the water drains away at increasing speed until it reaches a maximum about half way between high and low water; then it slows until it is zero again at low tide water. When the flood starts the flow increases to a maximum half way to high water and then slows down until slack water at high tide. The ratio of speeds are approximately as shown below.

State of Tide	High Water	HW + 1hr	HW + 2hrs	HW + 3hrs
Speed of Tidal Stream	0	1	2	3

State of Tide	HW + 4hrs	HW + 5hrs	Low Water
Speed of Tidal Stream	2	1	0

If you know this relationship and the maximum speed of the tide you can work out roughly how fast the tide will go at other times.

SPRING AND NEAP TIDES

The tidal flow is caused mainly by the gravitational pull of the moon but the pull of the sun also has an effect. When the sun and moon are in line with each other and the earth, at new moon and full moon, their combined pull gives the highest, and lowest, tides of the month. These are known as spring tides. When the moon is at right angles to the line joining the sun and earth, the smallest tides occur. These are known as neap tides.

RISE AND FALL

Because the rise and fall of water level is due to the movement of an enormous quantity of water the change in the level depends upon the shape of the land. In some places the rise is quite small, and in the Mediterranean and Baltic Seas it is hardly noticeable because the sea is too small for the moon to have much effect on it and the entrances are too narrow to allow much tidal water from the Atlantic Ocean to enter. The biggest effects are where a large ocean is funnelled into a small area. For example, at Avonmouth in the eastern part of the Bristol Channel the highest spring tides reach forty-five feet and the speeds reach five knots. However, most of Britain has ranges of a few feet and speeds of one or two knots. The causes of differences from place to place are very complex and you cannot hope to predict them. You must find out what to expect from tide tables.

Over hundreds of years data have been collected on the behaviour of the tides at various places round the coasts. These have enabled hydrographers to draw up tables to predict what the tide will be doing at any time in the future, not allowing for variations due to weather conditions. You can buy detailed tables for most ports and harbours but if you are interested in more than one place it is more convenient to buy a set of tables which give high water times at Dover for every day of the year and a list of 'tidal constants'. These constants are the time in hours and minutes which must be added to or subtracted from the time of high water at Dover to give the time of high water at the other ports and harbours in Britain. These times are always in Greenwich Mean Time so don't forget to allow for summer time when necessary. You can also buy charts which show the directions and speeds of the tidal flows round the British Isles. A nautical almanac, such as Reeds, contains much of this information. However, tidal charts are not very accurate close to the shore, where dinghies are likely to be sailing, and more accurate information can be gained from large-scale Admiralty charts which give rates and directions at several points for each hour after high water at the main port nearby.

There are a few points about the behaviour of tidal streams which are worth remembering. First, they run more strongly round headlands and more weakly in bays, as you would expect from the section on currents. In addition, a stream will set into a bay because the water is flooding in to fill it up. Third, it will turn first inshore and later offshore.

Tide races occur when the tide runs through a narrow channel and is therefore speeded up. Overfalls, or tide rips, occur when the sea bottom suddenly becomes shallower or where two tidal streams meet in opposition.

WEATHER EFFECTS

The height which the water actually reaches is not always exactly that predicted by the tide tables, because the weather can affect it. A strong wind blowing with the tide can make it reach a level even higher than predicted but when it is blowing against it it can hold it back. In addition, high barometric pressure tends to give lower tides, and low barometric pressure tends to give higher tides.

Winds

I do not propose to give a discourse on meteorology and weather forecasting as the subject is too complex to be covered in a few pages. However, you can find out what the experts forecast from various sources. There is an RYA booklet G5/77 called *Weather Forecasts*, which gives details of national forecasts broadcasting by the BBC Radio and a list of coastal stations which will give a local forecast by telephone. In addition, in most areas the GPO provides a recorded telephone broadcast.

There are a large number of rhymes which sailors have composed to help them forecast the weather. Here are the ones that I find useful. They are not, of course, infallible but are helpful.

The Barometer

1. Long foretold; long last
   Short warning; soon past
   Quick rise after low
   Indicates a stronger blow.

2. With a low and falling glass
   Soundly sleeps the careless ass.
   Only when its high and rising
   Truly rests the careful wise 'un.

Wind and Weather

1. Red sky at night, sailors delight
   Red sky in the morning, sailors warning.

2. Mackerel sky and mares tails
   Make lofty ships carry low sails.

3. When the wind shifts against the sun
   Trust it not for back it will run.

4. When the rain comes before the wind
   Halyards sheets and braces mind.
   When the wind comes before the rain
   Soon it will be fine again.

The behaviour of wind when it blows over sea and land when it is deflected by obstructions is similar to the behaviour of water. However,

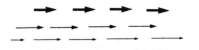

Fig 59 Wind blowing over a flat surface

Fig 60 Wind blowing over a hill

because air is less dense and can be compressed, unlike water, and is often moving much faster it is much more difficult to make precise predictions. Even so, every dinghy sailor should have some idea how wind is affected by circumstances.

FLAT SURFACES

When wind blows over a flat surface there is friction between the wind and the surface which slows down the lower layers of air. Friction is much greater between wind and land than between wind and sea, and generally the wind speed over land is only about half that over water.

When wind speeds at sea are quoted they are assumed to be measured at a height of 33 feet above sea level. The actual speed at sea level is about one third less than the speed at 33 feet.

HILLS AND VALLEYS

When air flows over hills the situation is rather like that when water is flowing round islands. The direction is changed and the speed tends to be increased over the hill with an eddy on the leeward side. If there are valleys in the direction of the wind it tends to blow strongly along them rather than over the hills. If the wind is blowing across a valley with hills to windward and leeward there is likely to be a circular eddy which will give a wind in the valley blowing in the opposite direction to the main wind, rather like the current in a bay.

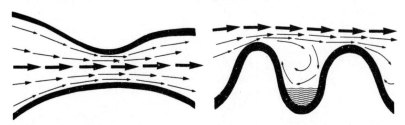

Fig 61 Bird's eye view of wind blowing along a valley

Fig 62 Wind blowing across a valley

81

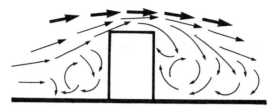

Fig 63 Wind blowing over an obstruction

OBSTRUCTIONS

An obstruction like a large building can affect the wind at quite a distance both to leeward and to windward as it breaks the smooth flow of wind and forms eddies. This situation often exists if you are launching from or returning to a jetty or sea wall and you will find the wind gusty and fickle.

If the obstruction is another sailing boat on the water the extent to which it affects the smooth flow of the wind depends on the set of the sails. A close-hauled boat produces turbulent wind for about three or four boat lengths to leeward while a boat running free with a spinnaker or sails goosewinged may upset the smooth flow for up to ten boat lengths.

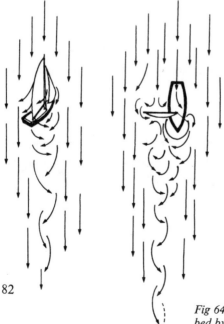

82

Fig 64 Bird's eye view of wind disturbed by sails

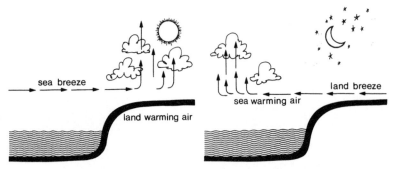

Fig 65 Formation of a sea breeze   *Fig 66 Formation of a land breeze*

THERMAL WINDS

When the sun shines on different surfaces it warms them up to differing degrees. The warmth of the surface warms the air over it, which rises, drawing in air from cooler parts. The most common thermal winds are land and sea breezes which occur because the land warms up and cools down more quickly than the sea, particularly on sunny days and cloudless nights.

In the day the sun warms the land more than the sea. The land warms the air above it, which rises, and its place is taken by cooler air from the sea which blows in over the coast—a sea breeze. At night the reverse happens. The land cools down more quickly than the sea, air rises over the sea and is replace by cooler air off the land—a land breeze.

The strength of a sea breeze depends on the difference in warmth of land and sea and will therefore be greatest on a sunny day and least on an overcast day. The breeze will become established about mid-morning and will die away as the sun sinks in the evening. In Britain a strong breeze may reach a speed of eight knots, force 3, and extend about five miles out to sea. In countries where the sun is hot and the land arid the wind may be considerably stronger and more extensive.

Just as the differing warmth of sea and land gives rise to sea and land breezes, changes in the surface of the land can give local thermal winds, on a smaller scale. These can be quite important for inland sailing on a calm sunny day. A smart helmsman can sometimes find a favourable wind which his competitors miss by looking at the type of land surface bordering the lake. As the strength of a thermal breeze will be greatest close to the land causing it, it may be worth sailing a course closer to shore than would otherwise be necessary.

Part Three

Introduction to Racing

Sooner or later most dinghy owners are going to be tempted into competition with other sailors even if this was not their main aim in buying a boat. It is an experience that every sailor should undergo, even if he is much more interested in cruising or pottering, as it is the best way to learn how to make the best of his boat. To watch experts in action at close quarters will give the novice far more knowledge about the way in which his boat should be handled than he will learn by himself. Indeed I would suggest that anyone who is seriously interested in the competitive aspects of dinghy racing should spend a season crewing for a more experienced helmsman before competing as a helmsman himself.

To take part in races you must be a member of a sailing club. The Royal Yachting Association publish a booklet listing all the clubs in Great Britain. It is called *Addresses of National Authorities: R.Y.A. Affiliated Clubs and Classes.* As I said in the introduction it is wise to choose your club before you choose your boat, unless you are dead set on a particular class of dinghy, as it is better to buy a boat of one of the classes sailed by your club. Most clubs sail several classes of dinghy of various levels of performance and you can discuss them with club members before committing yourself to one.

The racing of dinghies is taken very seriously by many people, so even if you are not seriously interested in it you should know the rules and etiquette of racing so that you do not spoil other people's pleasure by behaving incorrectly. In the next two chapters the basic rules and procedures are described and some elementary tactics are discussed. If you intend to be really involved in racing you should read some of the specialized books listed in the bibliography.

The object of sailing in a race is to complete the course faster than the other competitors, while obeying the rules, and so reach the finishing line first. Of course, more people lose races than win them but you should not be content to follow the leaders round the course; you must always be trying to make your boat go faster, to pick the best course and to out-think the opposition. Do not make the mistake of supposing that because you have little experience you cannot win. Some of the most experienced sailors rarely win and some novices proceed with great alacrity to the top of national and international racing.

One of the most important things when racing is to know what you are doing. Always make sure that you know what course you are to sail, so that, even if other people make mistakes, you will not. And always know the rules governing the behaviour of boats when racing: sailing at close quarters can be unnerving and if you are not absolutely certain of what you and the others are allowed to do you may lose by disqualification or advantage will be taken of your ignorance. You can expect other helmsmen to behave correctly and, if they do not, you must protest, but you cannot expect them to be kind.

Chapter 10

Rules and Procedures

Yacht and dinghy racing takes place all over the world under the International Yacht Racing Union (IYRU) rules. These cover all aspects of the behaviour of boats while racing and are very detailed, covering the most unlikely situations as well as the everyday ones. You can buy a copy of the IYRU rules from the Royal Yachting Association, but there are also a number of books on the market which explain the rules with diagrams. In this chapter I intend to explain only those rules which it is absolutely essential to know before entering a race as it takes a whole book to explain them all.

The rules cover two basic situations: boats meeting in open water and boats rounding marks. (A mark is the buoy or other object which defines a turning point of the race course.)

BOATS MEETING IN OPEN WATER

1. Boats on opposite tacks.
   Rule 36. A port tack yacht shall keep clear of a starboard tack yacht.
2. Boats on the same tack.
   Rule 37.1. A windward yacht shall keep clear of a leeward yacht.
   Rule 37.2. A yacht clear astern shall keep clear of a yacht clear ahead.
3. Boats tacking or gybing.
   Rule 41.1. A yacht which is either tacking or gybing shall keep clear of a yacht on a tack.
4. Luffing
   Rule 38.1. A yacht clear ahead or a leeward yacht may luff as she pleases . . .

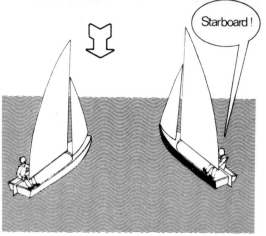

Fig 67 Starboard tack boat has right of way (Rule 36)

Fig 68 Leeward boat has right of way (Rule 37.1)

Fig 69 Boat astern keeps clear of boat ahead (Rule 37.2)

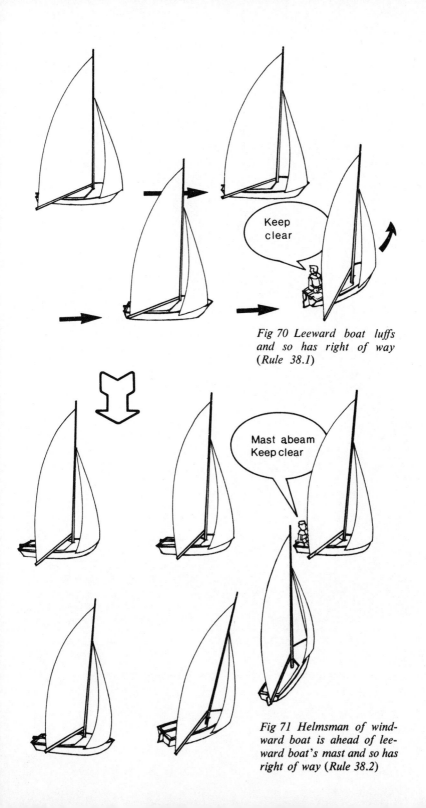

Fig 70 Leeward boat luffs and so has right of way (Rule 38.1)

Fig 71 Helmsman of windward boat is ahead of leeward boat's mast and so has right of way (Rule 38.2)

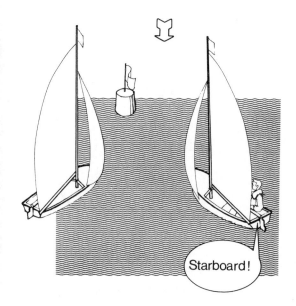

Fig 72 Approaching a mark starboard tack boat has right of way (Rule 36)

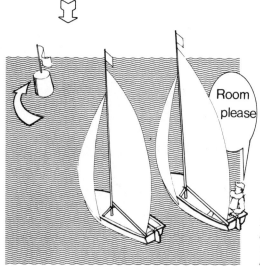

Fig 73 Approaching a mark an outside boat must make way for an overlapping inner boat (Rule 42.1a)

Fig 74 (Rule 42.1a)

Rule 38.2. A leeward yacht shall not sail above her proper course while an overlap exists if when the overlap began or at any time during its existence the helmsman of the windward yacht (when sighting abeam from his normal station and sailing no higher than the leeward yacht) has been abreast or forward of the mainmast of the leeward yacht.

Rule 40. Before the start the leeward yacht must luff slowly.

BOATS ROUNDING MARKS

A. At a windward mark.
1. When boats are on opposite tacks, Rule 36 (right of way to starboard tack boat) and Rule 41 (a boat tacking or gybing keeps clear of a boat on a tack) apply.
2. When boats are on the same tack.
   Rule 42.1a. An outside yacht shall give each yacht overlapping her on the inside room to round or pass the mark or obstruction. This rule does not apply when starting.
B. At an offwind mark.
1. Rule 42.1a (again). An outside yacht shall give each yacht overlapping her on the inside room to round or pass the mark or obstruction.

2. Rule 42.1a. A yacht clear astern shall keep clear in anticipation of and during the rounding or passing manoeuvre when the yacht clear ahead remains on the same tack or gybes.

These are the most important racing rules, but I say again that if you want to be really competitive you must get a copy of the entire rules and study them.

PROCEDURES

When you join a sailing club you will receive, among other things, a calendar of races. This will show you when there are races in your class on your piece of water and also when your club is sailing as guest of another club. Always arrive well before the time the race is due to start for you have a lot of things to do.

First of all, go to the clubhouse and notify the race committee that you intend to sail in the race. In a club race there will be no entry fee but if the race is open to all-comers there may be. Next, study the diagram which shows the course to be raced. If you can't understand it, ask a member of the race committee to explain. When you are sure you understand it copy it carefully on to a piece of paper or a piece of plastic laminate that will not go soggy if wet, together with the starting time and the signals to be used by the race committee. Make sure you know how many times you must sail the course and, if the race is shortened, what the signal is and what the shortened course is.

Having satisfied yourself that you are sure what the race consists of, prepare your boat. Rig it carefully, making sure that you have everything you need and, when it is rigged, inspect all the fittings, the buoyancy bags or compartments, and the hull. If the hull is dirty, wash it.

When you are ready to launch, return to the clubhouse to make sure that nothing to do with the race has been changed.

Launch about half-an-hour before the race is due to start so that you have time to get the feel of the boat and the weather. Make a few practice starts; decide which part of the starting line is set most favourably and time the approaches with a stopwatch so that you can arrive at the starting line when the starting signal is given.

Starting procedure is simple. Ten minutes before the start the flag used to identify your class of boat is broken out and a gun is fired to draw attention to it. The time at which the visual signal of the flag is broken out is crucial, not the sound of the gun. Five minutes before the start another specified flag is broken out and a gun again fired. The start takes place when the flags are lowered, a gun again being fired.

During the race your behaviour is governed by the racing rules. After you have crossed the finishing line, or if you have retired for any reason, get well away from boats still racing.

Chapter 11

Elementary Tactics

The race committee aims to set a course which will test the competitors on the three points of sailing, beating, reaching and running. The course is usually triangular with a long leg to windward, the beat, and shorter legs for reaching and running. Thus you will spend a large part of the race beating, which is generally considered to be the most testing sailing as regards both tactics and sheer boat speed.

THE START

Races are generally started to windward for two reasons. First, the boats are not moving so fast and can stop easily when close-hauled so there is less chance both of collision and of being over the starting line too soon. Second, the beat sorts the fleet out quickly so there is less likely to be congestion at the first mark.

Many race officers aim to set a starting line which is exactly at right angles to the wind so that boats starting at all points will be equally favoured. However, it is difficult to place the markers precisely and in any case the wind fluctuates in direction so that there is usually one end of the line which is slightly to windward of the other.

Sometimes the race committee will deliberately favour the port end of the line, setting it slightly to windward of the starboard end. As many boats like to start at the starboard end of the line on the starboard tack, which has right-of-way, so that they can bear away and sail along the line if they arrive too early, setting a line which favours the port end will encourage the fleet to spread out. This is very important if there is a large number of competitors.

The starboard tack start at the starboard end of the line is extremely popular because it is simple in conception. Unfortunately, it can be difficult in practice because there will be a lot of boats trying it so that the wind will be very disturbed. In addition you may find that you cannot bear away down the line if you are too early because a leeward boat may luff you and force you to slow right down to avoid collision with him. It may be better to decide where to start only when you have seen where the others are going. If you hang back a little way you should be able to get up speed and sail quickly into a gap, tacking if necessary, and pass the boats which have only dirty wind. It may well be a good idea to start at the port end so that you can sail slightly freer and faster on starboard tack than the pack who have started close together.

If you actually touch the mark you must sail right round it until you can start legitimately.

Starting is exciting and a good start can give you a tremendous lift while a start right in the midle of the fleet can give you intricate problems to solve.

THE WINDWARD LEG

As soon as you have started you must try to work yourself into a position where you have clear wind—wind which has not been disturbed by other boats. In addition, you can try to give your dirty wind to someone else to slow him down. Remember that each time you tack you lose a few seconds so don't tack unless you are sure it is necessary.

Because the direction of the wind is liable to fluctuate considerably there is usually one tack which will take you closer to the windward mark than the other. Try to get on this favourable tack and if the wind direction changes so that the other tack is favoured tack as soon as you can. It is not a good idea to try to reach the windward mark in two long tacks as a wind shift may leave you hopelessly to leeward of the mark. Tack when there is a good reason for doing so—to get clear wind, to give your dirty wind to a close competitor, to take advantage of a wind shift or because you can now lay a course to round the mark. Try not to let an opponent force you into tacking when you don't want to. Pass behind a right-of-way boat rather than putting about on to his tack.

Avoid trying to overtake a boat closely to windward as you will find a patch of dirty wind just to windward of his bows which will slow you down enough to stop you getting past.

As you approach the windward mark decide how you are going to round it. If you join a procession of boats rounding on the safe starboard tack you will get a lot of dirty wind which may force you to put in an extra short tack to avoid going the wrong side of the mark. Such an extra tack can be disastrous as you are then on port tack and have lost your place in the queue. So make sure that you have sailed far enough on the previous port tack before making a starboard tack approach. It may well be worth sailing quite a lot further on the port tack so that you can make a fast approach on a slightly freer course in clear wind. If you approach the mark on the port tack you will have to be quick to squeeze round it in a gap. Such gaps do not appear very often in large fleets.

OFFWIND LEGS

When you have rounded the windward mark you will usually find that the next leg is a broad reach. The course you choose to take depends on the speed of your boat on different points of sailing. You must decide if it is worth sailing a longer curved course so that you gain extra speed by having clear air away from the rest of the fleet. If you have a planing dinghy clear air may make the difference between planing and not planing.

If you decide to take a longer route you have a choice between sailing to leeward or windward of the fleet. If you sail to windward you get clear air but have to bear away at the end to reach the mark, which will give you a slow approach. If you sail to leeward you will have to go a lot further to avoid all the dirty wind from the other boats but you have the advantage of approaching the mark closer to the wind and therefore faster than the others.

THE GYBING MARK

It is important to start your turn early when gybing round the mark so that you are close to the mark as you leave it and to windward of the other boats.

THE RUN

The race committee will quite often include a dead run in the race by bringing boats directly back from the windward mark to the leeward mark on alternate laps of the course. It is important to remember that a boat does not sail very fast on a dead run. In fact, it is often worth taking a zig-zag course, tacking downwind, to keep the wind far enough round on the quarter to give more efficient sailing. The problem is to judge how much to zig-zag. This will depend on the strength of the wind and the speed characteristics of your boat. In multihulls, which sail very much faster on a reach, it is worth sailing a much longer course but in low-performance dinghies there may be no gain.

When on a dead run your speed is limited by the wind speed. Your sails will blanket the wind from another boat quite a long way ahead and you can slow another boat down by deliberately sailing astern of him. However, it is usually better to make your own way to the leeward mark, trying to catch favourable puffs of wind or a bit of extra current. There is little scope for tactical duels because the fleet will be spread out and moving slowly relative to one another.

THE LEEWARD MARK

As boats approach the leeward mark they will be converging on a number of courses, having spread out on the run. If there are a lot of boats rounding, get as close to the buoy as you can so that no other boat can force you out, but if there is room take a wide approach so that you can luff up sharply close to the mark and to windward of more careless boats.

THE FINISH

Like starting lines, finishing lines are rarely exactly across the wind or exactly to windward of the last mark so there will be a favourable end for finishing. However, because the markers at the two ends of the line are usually different sizes, often the committee boat and a buoy, it can be difficult to judge just how the line is laid. Watch any boats finishing before you and the apparent movement of the marker against the shore to try to judge which is nearer.

Always tack towards the end of the line you can lay first, but try to avoid wind shadow from a large committee boat. As you approach the line make sure there are no boats which will prevent you tacking to lay the line. Get away from them before you are caught and forced to overstand the mark.

When you have crossed the line, get away from it quickly so that you do not interfere with boats finishing after you.

Glossary of Nautical Terms

Abeam	at the side of the boat, at right angles to the direction it is facing
Aft	at or towards the stern
Battens	thin, flat pieces of wood or plastic used to stiffen a sail to help it keep a good shape
Beating	sailing as nearly into the wind as possible
Bermuda sail	a tall triangular sail whose whole luff is attached to the mast
Bearing away	changing course so that the boat is heading further away from the direction from which the wind is blowing
Bilge water	water which has been splashed or leaked into the bottom of the boat
Block	a pulley, through which a rope can run smoothly while under load
Boltrope	a rope sewn into the edge of a sail to strengthen it
Boom	a horizontal pole used to extend the foot of a sail
Bow	the front of a boat
Buoyancy	the tendency of a lighter-than-water body to rise to the surface of the water
Burgee	a small triangular flag (square for racing) flown at the masthead to indicate the wind direction
Centreboard	a flat board or plate which can be lowered through a slot in the hull to reduce sideways movement of the boat
Cleat	a fitting with one or, usually, two horns round which a rope is hitched
Clevis pin	a metal pin with a head at one end and a hole drilled through the other through which a pin or ring can be put to keep the clevis pin in position
Clew	the aft corner of a sail
Cockpit	the open part of the boat behind the mast in which the crew sits

Critical speed	the maximum speed to be expected from a boat floating in water, equal to 1.2 L where L is the waterline length
Fairlead	a fitting with a smooth hole through which a rope passes
Foot	the lowest side of a sail
Forestay	the rigging line from the mast to the bows
Forward	at or towards the bows of the boat
Frictional resistance	the resistance to movement of the boat due to the drag of the water on the hull
Gooseneck	a fitting which attaches the boom to the mast while allowing it to pivot freely
Goosewinged	sailing downwind with the mainsail on one side of the boat and the jib on the other
Gybe	a change of course during which the boat presents her stern to the wind and the mainsail and boom are blown from one side of the boat to the other
Halyard	a rope used to hoist a sail up the mast
Hanks	fittings which attach the jib luff to the forestay
Head	the top corner of a sail
Heel	the angle from the vertical made by the boat when the wind pushes her over sideways
In irons	head to wind and stationary
In stays	the position during tacking when the boat is head to wind and the sails are not filling
Jam cleat	a ridged sprung slot into which a rope can be jammed to hold it taut
Jib	a triangular sail set on the forestay
Jib stick	a pole used to hold the jib out from the mast while running; sometimes called a whisker pole
Kicking strap	a rope from the boom to the base of the mast which prevents the boom from lifting too high
Knot	one nautical mile per hour i.e. 6080 feet per hour
Leach	the back edge of a sail
Leeward	the direction to which the wind is blowing e.g. the leeward boat is the one which the wind reached last
Leeway	the angle between the direction in which a boat is pointing and the course she is actually making due to being pushed sideways as well as forwards by the wind
Luff (1)	the front edge of a sail
Luff (2)	to change course so that the boat is heading nearer to the direction from which the wind is blowing
Mast	a vertical pole held up by rigging which supports the sails
Pinching	sailing a boat so close to the wind that the speed decreases
Planing	when a boat is no longer moving through the water but is lifted hydrodynamically on to the surface and can reach greater speeds

Port	left when looking forward in a boat
Quarter	the side of a boat near the stern
Reaching	sailing with the wind abeam
Residual resistance	the resistance of the water to being pushed aside by the boat
Rudder	a board suspended vertically at the stern which, when moved, steers the boat
Running	sailing with the wind coming from astern
Self-bailers	devices which protrude through the hull and use the motion of the boat to suck out bilge water
Sheet	a rope which controls the position of a sail by pulling the clew
Shrouds	rigging lines from the mast to the sides of the boat
Slot effect	the effect of the jib in funnelling air over the mainsail giving increased power
Spinnaker	an approximately hemispherical sail which is attached to the boat only by its corners
Spinnaker guy	rope running from the windward quarter of the boat to the tack of the spinnaker
Spinnaker sheet	a rope running from the leeward quarter of the boat to the clew of the spinnaker
Stability	the tendency of a boat to return to its normal, rest position
Starboard	right when looking forward in a boat
Stern	the back of the boat
Tack (1)	the forward corner of a sail
Tack (2)	a change of course during which the bows point directly into the wind
Tacking	travelling into the wind in a series of zig-zags
Thwart	a seat across the boat
Tiller	a pole attached to the top of the rudder with which the helmsman steers the boat
Toe straps	long wide straps attached to the bottom of the boat for the crew to hook their feet under to prevent them falling out
Transom	the flat vertical plank across the stern of a dinghy
Trapeze	a wire from high up the mast which a crew can clip to a harness enabling him to lean out horizontally with his feet on the side of the boat
Trim	the position a boat takes up in the water
Wetted area	the surface area of a boat's hull which is in contact with the water
Whisker pole	jib stick
Windward	the direction from which the wind is blowing e.g. the windward side of a boat is the one that the wind reaches first

Appendix

Table 1 Beaufort wind scale with sea, land and dinghy equivalents

Beaufort Number	Wind Speed in knots	Description	Sea	Land	Dinghy
0	less than 1	calm	sea like a mirror	smoke rises vertically	becalmed
1	1-3	light air	ripples like scales but without foam crests	wind direction shown by smoke but not by wind vanes	helmsman and crew sit on opposite sides of boat going to windward
2	4-6	light breeze	small wavelets; crests do not break	Wind felt on face; leaves rustle; vanes moved by wind	helmsman and crew both sit to windward
3	7-10	gentle breeze	large wavelets; crests begin to break; foam of glassy appearance; scattered white horses	leaves and twigs in constant motion; light flag extended	helmsman and crew sit on windward gunwale
4	11-16	moderate breeze	small waves, becoming larger; fairly frequent white horses	raises dust and loose paper; small branches move	helmsman and crew lean out hard or use trapeze
5	17-21	fresh breeze	moderate waves taking a more pronounced long form; many white horses	small trees in leaf begin to sway	most racing dinghies ease sheets in heavier gusts
6	22-27	strong breeze	large waves begin to form; white foam crest extensive everywhere	large branches in motion; telephone wires whistle; umbrellas difficult to use	only well-reefed dinghies can sail

Further Reading

DINGHIES FOR ALL WATERS, Eric Coleman. *Hollis and Carter*
GETTING AFLOAT, Annually, *Link House Publications*
SAILING FROM START TO FINISH, Yves-Louis Pinaud, 1975. *Adlard Coles Ltd.*
SAIL RACER, Jack Knights, 1973. *Adlard Coles Ltd.*
SMALL BOAT RACING, James B Moore, 1967, *Stanley Paul*
SMALL BOAT RACING WITH THE CHAMPIONS, Ed. Bob Fisher, 1976, *Barrie and Jenkins*
NEW GLENANS SAILING MANUAL, THE. 1978. *David and Charles*

For a catalogue of RYA booklets write to RYA Publications, Shaftesbury Road, Gillingham, Dorset, SP8 4LJ

Index